Go to Work on
Your Career

First published in Great Britain in 2001 by
Go MAD Books
Pocket Gate Farm
Off Breakback Road
Woodhouse Eaves
Leicestershire
LE12 8RS

British Library Cataloguing in Publication Data.
A catalogue record for this book is available from the British Library.

ISBN 0-9537284-4-7

Printed and bound in Great Britain by Bath Press, Bath

ACKNOWLEDGEMENTS

There are many people we would like to thank for their contributions, feedback, stories, willingness to help, encouragement and inspiration that enabled this book to come into being. Specifically we would like to mention:

Professor David Wilson at Warwick University for his help, advice and guidance in the early stages of this project, and we are particularly grateful for his support and encouragement.

The people we have interviewed in the process of researching and writing this book. You were all great and make our jobs that extra bit special. We feel privileged to have met so many fascinating and inspiring individuals. Very special thanks to you all for sharing your career stories and providing us with a wealth of material.

All the organisations that contributed to this research. In particular we would like to express our appreciation to the following:

Acordis Acetates
One2One
Royal and SunAlliance
RS Components

All the participants of our Go to Work on Your Career programmes who have given us endless examples and experiences to draw on in creating a book on career management.

The rest of the Go MAD® team, our families and friends – you all know who you are – what would we do without you? Thanks for the tireless support, endless encouragement, hard work, amazing ideas and just for being there.

Contents

Page

ACKNOWLEDGEMENTS

INTRODUCTION

1.	Welcome to Go to Work on Your Career	11
2.	Whose career is it anyway?	13
3.	Learn how to lay crazy paving	13
4.	It's people who make the difference	14
5.	Learn from others	15
6.	More about the book	16
7.	Ways to approach the book	19
8.	How well do you plan your holidays?	20
9.	In case you are not convinced	20

DEFINE YOUR CAREER

10.	Decide your own definition	23
11.	Manage consciously or unconsciously	24
12.	How are you managing?	28
13.	Have a strategy	29
14.	The only way isn't up	31

FIND YOUR REASON WHY

The story of Margaret Burke		33
15.	For the right reasons	34
16.	Discover reasons for managing your career	37
17.	Give added value to your motivation	39
18.	Measure your passion	40
19.	Identify the direction you are moving in	42
20.	Make your reason stronger	43
21.	Remind yourself to keep going	44

DECIDE WHAT IS IMPORTANT TO YOU

The story of Sarah Armitage		47
22.	Determine your values	49

23.   Value your values   52
24.   Align your values   52
25.   Love the work you do   53
26.   Determine your own success   54
27.   Recognise your life priorities   55
28   Build your picture of what is important to you   57
29.   Go for job satisfaction   60

ACHIEVE A BALANCE

The story of Carl Robley   65
30.   Find the balance   67
31.   Be a balancing act   67
32.   Get the right balance   69
33.   Measure the quality   70
34.   Act like you mean it   71
35.   Be realistic   72
36.   Manage the pressure   72
37.   Take control of your pressure   73
38.   Have a cut-off point   75
39.   Keep the balance   76

CONTRIBUTION FROM ONE2ONE   79

DEFINE YOUR GOALS

The story of Helen Bunbury   81
40.   Decide to make a decision about what you want   82
41.   Identify areas for goal setting   83
42.   Explore your reason why   86
43.   Aspire to achieve   87
44.   Ignore the "Yes Buts"   88
45.   Enjoy the journey   89
46.   What to do when you don't know what to do   90
47.   Put your goals in writing   91
48.   Use the power of your mind   93
49.   Programme your mind   94
50.   State your goals positively   95
51.   Think to the future   95
52.   Remind yourself   97
53.   Give yourself positive messages   97

54.	Believe it is true	98
55.	Chunk down	98
56.	Involve others	99
57.	Not set in concrete	100
58.	Keep them rolling	100
59.	Dare to be different	101

BELIEVE IN YOURSELF

The story of Darren Brooker		105
60.	Know yourself	106
61.	Develop your self-awareness	107
62.	Identify your beliefs	108
63.	Make your beliefs work with you	110
64.	Have good conversations with yourself	111
65.	Identify all the positives about your career	114
66.	Turn the shoulds into coulds	115
67.	Ask yourself high quality questions	116
68.	Have enabling beliefs	118
69.	Build your own beliefs	120
70.	Affirm your beliefs	120
71.	Build your confidence	122
72.	Prepare to be confident	124
73.	Focus on the positive	124
74.	Talk with confidence	125
75.	Find a role model	126
76.	Take small risks	127
77.	Learn from experience	128
78.	Get the butterflies flying in formation	128
CONTRIBUTION FROM ROYAL AND SUNALLIANCE		131

DEVELOP YOUR ABILITIES

The story of Nigel Beard		133
79.	Personal development and career management	134
80.	Continue to develop	135
81.	Assess your current abilities	136
82.	Review your personal goals	142
83.	Seek support from your organisation	144
84.	Involve others by observing excellence	145

85.   Evaluate what organisations want   146
86.   Develop transferable skills   148
87.   Be prepared for the future   150
88.   Consider opportunities and threats   152
89.   Identify ways to develop   154
90.   Choose the most appropriate development activity   156
91.   Keep a record of your abilities and achievements   156

CONTRIBUTION FROM ELECTROCOMPONENTS   161

BUILD A SUPPORT NETWORK

The story of Ken Bew   163
92.   Recognise the need for support   165
93.   Seek support for different needs   166
94.   Ask for help   169
95.   Be your own coach   169
96.   Show appreciation   170
97.   Give in return   170

CREATE OPPORTUNITIES

The story of Mark Christer   175
98.   Be proactive   176
99.   Remember you always have a choice   177
100. Identify your choices   178
101. Take control of your career   178
102. Be career responsible   179
103. Consider the worst that could happen   182
104. Become a surveyor and a proposer   185
105. Make homework a habit   189
106. Make the most of opportunities   191

CONTRIBUTION FROM ACORDIS ACETATES   193

MARKET YOURSELF

The story of Rebecca Denning-Southern   195
107. Stand out from the crowd   196
108. Identify the right people   196
109. Make the most of indirect contacts   198

110.	Map out your relationships	199
111.	Get noticed for the right reasons	203
112.	Stray from the norm	204
113.	Be a volunteer	205
114.	Add value	206
115.	Network, network and network	207
116.	Identify opportunities for networking	208
117.	Take eight steps to successful networking	210
118.	Expand your net	213
119.	Develop a script	213
120.	Introduce yourself to create interest	214
121.	Present a positive image	216

TELL YOUR STORY

The story of Brigideen McGuire		221
122.	Reflect on the past	224
123.	Look to the future	226

PLAN YOUR WAY FORWARD

The story of Mike Waterfield		229
124.	Pull it all together	230
125.	Continue to learn from others	231
126.	Review before planning	232
127.	Review your reason why	233
128.	Reflect on what is important to you	234
129.	Go for a balanced life	235
130.	Identify your key goal areas	236
131.	Write down your goals	237
132.	Identify possibilities	238
133.	Prioritise and plan	240
134.	Go to Work on Your Career Action Plan	240
135.	Ensure it happens	244
136.	Time to say goodbye	244
137.	Find the actions that relate to you	246
138.	Index of stories	250
139.	Go MAD® information	252

Go to Work on Your Career

INTRODUCTION

1. Welcome to Go to Work on Your Career

Just in case you haven't noticed, the first thing to do is to let you know that three people have written this book. As there are three authors we will be using the royal 'we' throughout the book. We have written this introduction section to let you know who we are; explain why and how the book came into being; tell you who the book is for; and suggest ways you might choose to approach using the book.

We should also let you know that this book is easy to read, and the style may even appear a fraction more informal than other career management books you have come across (if you have read any career management books before). This is intentional; we wanted to create a book that you could read as if someone was talking to you, rather than at you. Hopefully, a bit like having a conversation with a friend!

**"One learns through the heart,
not the eyes or the intellect."
Mark Twain**

So, who are Andy, Kathryn and Nicky?

We are a team of consultants from Go MAD Ltd, a company which specialises in helping people to understand and develop their ability to make a difference. We achieve this by: undertaking research projects; providing training and coaching solutions; and providing help, guidance and support to organisations through a range of text, audio and I.T. based development materials.

In 1996 Andy, with years of experience in organisational change, training and consultancy, found himself in a career

11

rut. He had just completed the dissertation of his Masters degree in Human Resource Development. His dissertation focused on how people managed, or mismanaged, their careers. Andy came to the realisation that he wasn't actually managing his career. It was at this stage that he founded Career Strategies Ltd (which has now evolved into Go MAD Ltd), to fulfil his personal goals and align his work with the differences that he wanted to make. As the company name suggests, a key aspect was helping organisations and individuals to determine and implement their career management strategies.

Kathryn joined Career Strategies Ltd six months later, after making a career decision to continue to use her vast experience in training and development in a different environment. She was looking to work in a less hierarchical organisation that cared for her as an individual and allowed her the freedom to make good use of her abilities. Andy and Kathryn drew on their knowledge and experience of career management to develop the *Go to Work on Your Career* programme, which provided us with the title of this book. This programme has been successfully running since 1997, with people attending either on an individual basis, or as corporate groups. We decided to call the programme, and the book, *Go to Work on Your Career* because this is what we want to achieve; to encourage, inspire and cajole people into putting some work into their careers.

And last but not least Nicky joined Andy, Kathryn and others in the Go MAD® team to bring expertise in the areas of research and psychology. Nicky, having trained as a nurse, had reached a stage where she was facing some life changes. She decided to give up paid work to study and pursue her dreams to become qualified in the area of psychology. She now fulfils a role which makes excellent use of her abilities and allows her, as she says, *"To have a job where I don't feel like I'm going to work."*

> **"Your work is to discover your work and then with
> all your heart to give yourself to it."**
> **Buddha**

So, three of us have been involved in researching, writing
and producing the book. Three people who have followed
different career paths, and applied different strategies. We
will share more of our experiences in this book through
personal examples of our own career management. We will
also share with you examples, hints, tips and strategies
applied by the many people we have met over the years as
we have helped them to go to work on their careers.

2.   Whose career is it anyway?

This book is for anyone and everyone who might want to
reflect on what they do with their time at work (and also
the time out of work). It is for people who are happy in
their current job; people who are looking for something
different; people still searching for that elusive career that
will make their life and work meaningful; and people who
would like to be happier at work. For those individuals
who realise, or would like to realise, that they can have a
say in their careers and what they do in their working
hours. People who would like to well and truly go to work
on their careers.

Above all, this book is for people who answer the question,
whose career is it anyway with a loud and clear *MINE!*

3.   Learn how to lay crazy paving

> **"There is no such thing as a career path. It is crazy
> paving and you have to lay it yourself."**
> **Dominic Cadbury**

This book will help you to lay your crazy paving, wherever you may be on your career path. It is about you realising the influence you can have over your career. This might be laying the first few slabs or putting the finishing touches to a fantastic mosaic.

4.   It's people who make the difference

When deciding to write a book about careers it made sense to look at how others go about managing their careers. So, to build on previous research, and our career management experience of working with companies and individuals, this book is based on a specific research project undertaken to explore how individuals go to work on their careers. We approached organisations and asked them to nominate people who they felt were making a difference in the way they managed their careers.

"Things do not get better by being left alone."
Winston Churchill

By now, you will probably have already noticed that we talk a lot about *Making A Difference*. This isn't by accident; it is something that is close to our hearts. As well as the career management research which enabled us to write this book, we have spent the last five years researching how individuals apply a natural success process to make a difference, or Go MAD® (Make A Difference) as we call it. Hence, the change of company name to Go MAD Ltd.

From this ongoing research, a process based upon seven success principles has been identified which underpins the differences that people make. The specific research for this book, Go to Work on Your Career, is different to our ongoing research as it focused purely on career management. However, it was evident that the people we interviewed in the research for this book were applying these same principles, either consciously or unconsciously. So, although they won't be presented to you as a list, the principles of Go MAD® underpin the many strategies, tips and techniques presented in this book. The Go MAD® process and principles are explained in depth in Andy's book "Go MAD – The Art of Making A Difference."

The individuals nominated to be involved in the research for Go to Work on Your Career were managing their careers in a way that made differences, big and small, to themselves, their organisation, their work, and their life. The people involved in the research are not necessarily 'high-fliers', but people who have been determined, and brave enough, to make the decision to actively choose to get where they wanted to be, and where they are now. This wasn't just about making a difference for themselves - the research highlighted how those who were proactively managing their careers were having a positive impact on those they worked with and the organisations they worked for.

"Is there anyone so wise as not to learn from the experience of others."
Voltaire

By carrying out in-depth interviews with each of the individuals nominated we were able to gather evidence of career paths trodden, strategies employed, techniques used, actions taken, obstacles overcome and principles applied. This book will share all this material with you so that you can use it to get to where you want to be – or decide where it is you are going.

5. Learn from others

Quite often, career paths are well trodden and worn and, as we have already said, this book will give you the opportunity to learn how others have gone to work on their careers. The sections in the book start with a personal story – the story of how someone else has managed an element, an area, or the whole of their career.

Whatever stage you have reached in your career there will be stories you can relate to; stories that get you thinking about your approach to your career; and stories to inspire you to want to get up and do something – something that may be large or small, something that can make a difference and help you to feel happier at work.

The book also contains contributions from key people at some of the organisations in which the research took place. They will share with you an organisational perspective on career management. Although the ultimate responsibility for managing your career lies with you, you will not be doing this in isolation from the organisation you work in. Whilst managing your career you may well be looking to your organisation to provide opportunities or support, and obviously they will be looking for you to give something in return. How your organisation supports or encourages you, and your career development, will impact on the decisions you take while managing your career.

6. More about the book

Each personal story will emphasise a number of points vital in successfully going to work on your career. Following each story these points will be highlighted, and expanded on, so that you can get an understanding of how you might apply others' successes to your own situation. These learning points will then be built on with activities and questions for you to ask yourself. They will help you to think through how you currently manage your career and determine whether you might want to manage it differently.

Go to Work on Your Career is not intended to be the ultimate comprehensive career guide, but a thought provoking and practical 'doing' book. We mentioned earlier that we hoped you would feel like you are having a conversation with a friend. At times, we hope this book will challenge you to take time to focus on you and your career; to ask yourself thought provoking questions; to think about what you are currently doing; and to plan for the future.

**"This is a world of action and not for
moping and groaning in."
Charles Dickens**

We encourage you to do all the activities, which will mean writing in the spaces provided in the book. So make sure you have a pen or pencil handy. Be brave enough to jot down your thoughts – it's your book and it's your career.

Obviously, it's your choice whether you do or don't do the activities. However, the act of writing will ensure you think in depth about the points we raise. The thought processes involved in having to think in enough depth to do activities, or write down answers to questions, will really get you going to work on your career.

Quite often, when we say we don't need to physically do something (for example, pick up a pen and do the activities in this book), and that we will *think* about it instead, what we are really saying is we can't be bothered. If you're not bothered about doing some activities that will help you consider how you currently manage your career, and how you could approach your career differently, who else is going to be bothered for you?

If you don't want to write in the book because others might look at it (pass it around, discuss it with friends, or disagree with what you have written), then use separate sheets of paper to respond to the activities and questions.

Interspersed throughout the book, gathered from a variety of sources, are some of our favourite inspirational quotes relating to the points covered in each section. Some you may agree with, some you may not. The intention is that you give them some thought. Perhaps they might prompt some ideas or start to mean something for you on a personal level. Or it could be that some really appeal to you and you start to gather your own favourite quotes.

Here's one that particularly appeals to us:

**"To love what you do and feel that it matters –
how could anything be more fun?"
Katherine Graham**

Each section will end by giving you the opportunity to capture your thoughts. Thoughts that have been provoked by reading the personal stories, reflecting on questions put to you, or resulting from the activities you undertake. We have included this activity so that you have a summary of the points raised for you from each section that you work through.

Also, at the end of each section we will suggest three actions you can take to help you to Go to Work on Your Career. These actions will relate to the points covered in that section. The intention is to give you practical suggestions to transfer your learning from the pages of the book to the real world. It may be that you are already doing some or all of these actions. Some might not appeal to you in the least, and some you will want to go and do straight away. Use them as prompts and take forward those that appeal, and will work for you.

**"Keep going and the chances are you will stumble on
something, perhaps when you are least expecting it.
I have never heard of anyone stumbling on
something sitting down."
Charles F. Kettering**

The last section in the book, titled **PLAN YOUR WAY FORWARD**, gives you the opportunity to put together your own Go to Work on Your Career Action Plan. This will give you the chance to pull together everything from the book that struck a cord with you. It will also act as a reminder of things you want to do to move your career forward.

7. Ways to approach the book

As with most things there is more than one approach you can take to get the most out of this book. Having just encouraged you to do the activities, we will also mention that not every learning point or activity will be relevant for every person reading this book. What is relevant for you will depend on how you are currently feeling about the state of your career, your current work situation, and the strategies that you already use in managing your career.

"What is right for one soul may not be right for another. It may mean having to stand on your own and do something strange in the eyes of others."
Eileen Caddy

The following points highlight the different ways you may wish to approach this book:

- Read it all through first, highlighting the activities that will be meaningful for you. Then go back and do the activities, either in one go or over a period of time.

- Read through the whole book, doing all the activities.

- At the back of the book (pages 246-249) there is a list of the actions that are suggested at the end of each section. Refer to the list to see which ones grab your attention. Then you can just read the sections relating to those actions, doing the relevant activities.

- Dip in and out of the book in any order.

You may find that you think of a different approach to take. It doesn't matter which way you choose as long as it works for you.

8. How well do you plan your holidays?

Over the years, through our work in career management, either running workshops and programmes, or working with people on a one to one basis, we have come to realise how little time people give to planning their careers.

In fact, we consider that on average most people spend more time planning their yearly holiday than they spend thinking about or planning their careers. Does this ring true for you?

By reading and doing the activities in this book you will be putting yourself in the small percentage of the population who give some time and thought as to what they want from their working life. If you complete the Go to Work on Your Career Action Plan you will be putting yourself in an even smaller percentage of the population – those who actually plan and write down what they want from their careers. We want to let you into a secret – you deserve it. You deserve to decide what makes you happy at work, where you want to go, and what you want to get out of all those hours you spend in the workplace.

"NOT I, NOT ANYONE else can travel that road for you. You must travel it for yourself."
Walt Whitman

---

9. In case you are not convinced

If you still need convincing that active career management might be worthwhile for you – consider the following:

11 Reasons to Go to Work on Your Career

- It's no one else's responsibility.

- To ensure your career is what you want it to be.

- To keep developing, in order to remain employable in a changing world.

- Because your existing knowledge and skills are becoming outdated as each day passes.

- To maintain and develop transferable skills.

- Because you cannot rely on an employer for job security.

- To increase your value in the workplace.

- To focus on what is **really** important to you.

- Because what you do at work impacts on your life outside of work.

- To increase your job satisfaction without changing jobs.

- Because you are important and your working hours make up a large percentage of your life.

And finally remember-

"Many men go fishing all their lives without knowing that it is not the fish they are after."
Henry David Thoreau

So, enjoy the personal stories, enjoy the book, discover some more about you and your career, and above all ....
Go to Work on Your Career!

"The average length of a job has hardly changed over the last ten years in Britain or America, remaining constant at around six years. A full-time career is, therefore, a succession of six-year jobs."
Charles Handy

DEFINE YOUR CAREER

10. Decide your own definition

Before we start to look at the stories of others and ways of managing your career, let's take a moment to establish what we actually mean when we are talking about a 'career' and 'career management'.

As you get further into the book, and read through the personal examples of the careers of the individuals featured, it will become apparent that they have different definitions of what a career is. Our work, with thousands of individuals, has shown that there are many definitions and thoughts about what a career means on a personal level. These include: progress through promotion; being happy at work; increased job satisfaction; continually learning and developing; achieving work-life balance; being their own boss; and that a career is not just what they do at work but how they want to live their life.

Therefore, when working with groups or individuals we don't tend to use a specific career definition, instead we work with individuals' own definitions of a career.

PICK UP YOUR PEN

Give yourself the opportunity to consider your definition of a career. Before we start to focus on how you manage your career, stop and think about what this word 'career' means for you.

Use the space on the following page to note down your definition of a career.

This is the first time we have asked you to pick up your pen – so give it go!

23

My definition of a career is:

Obviously we don't know what you have written. However, we have identified two common distinctions; firstly, you may consider a career focuses on how you progress and develop through your work or, alternatively, you may feel that your career encompasses your life outside of paid work. Go to Work on Your Career will mainly focus on managing your career in a work context. However, at times in the book, we will reflect on how what you do in your working time, impacts on what you do outside of work. We will also encourage you to think about your balance of life between work and home.

Definition of a career:
"A person's course or progress through life."
Shorter Oxford Dictionary

11.   Manage consciously or unconsciously

Having reflected on your definition of a career, let's take the next step. Let's consider what it actually means to manage your career, in fact, what it means to Go to Work on Your Career!

Whether you realise it or not you have probably been managing your career in some way up to now. Sometimes this can be difficult to recognise because it may have been unconscious management through choices and decisions made. For others, this may be easy to see because their career management will have been actioned at a more conscious level, perhaps involving personal goals and well-planned steps.

**"I see my career as a limitless exploration of what life and the world has to offer. Continually developing and discovering new opportunities."
Career Management Workshop**

Let us give you an example of three people who participated in one of our Go to Work on Your Career programmes. These three individuals were very different in the way they had planned and managed their careers up to that point.

Geoff didn't feel that he managed his career. He had taken a job because that was all there was on offer at the time. He had several moves within the same company; all instigated by his employer. He was now in a job that he neither particularly liked nor disliked. He felt that things had just happened to him. He was participating in the programme because his company had suggested he came along to help him to think about what he wanted to do next.

Then there was Julie who had gone from opportunity to opportunity as they arose and was fairly happy with what she was doing. However, she had no idea what she wanted to do next. Her career management consisted of short-term focus, and whether she 'fancied' what was on offer. However, what she did recognise was that she was the one making the decisions and consequently determining what happened in her career. Julie wanted some time to reflect on what to do next, and wondered if she could be more proactive in her decision making.

And there was William, who had a ten-year plan of where he wanted to be in his organisation and how he was going to get there. William wanted to ensure that his ten-year plan was what he really wanted and that he wasn't restricting himself too much.

Julie and William realised that they were the ones who were having the impact on their careers. That it was their responsibility. Whereas Geoff had a differing viewpoint. Like other people we have come across, he felt that he had no control over his career or what he had chosen to do so far. In fact, he felt that he had little choice over the future. Because of this he hadn't bothered to think about his career in any depth. Participating in the programme was the first time he had thought about what he might want from his career.

**"Man is not the creature of circumstance.
Circumstances are the creatures of men."
Benjamin Disraeli**

We believe that managing your career does not necessarily mean that you have to have a structured plan that covers your whole life. However, if you want to be serious about managing your career, it does require some conscious thought. The thought you put into your career may be a long-term plan, or it may be about conscious decisions to take, or make, opportunities. This conscious thought will involve you regularly giving yourself time to consider your career, in order for you to determine how satisfied you are with where you are and where you want to be.

We regularly describe career management as being aware of:

- How I am reacting to my present circumstances.
- How I am creating my future.
- How I am aligning my work with my values and sense of identity.

This takes into account and brings together three key areas: making the most of what is happening at any time; putting some effort into making things happen; and reviewing how this fits with what is important to you as an individual. Consequently, if you give some thought to these three areas on a regular basis you are forming a good base point for managing your career.

"It is good to have an end to journey towards; but it is the journey that matters in the end."
Ursula Le Guin

Refer back to the three people used as an example in this section and consider how much conscious thought they were giving to their careers. On a career management conscious thinking scale of 1 to 10, William was at 10 on the scale! He had thought long and hard, and had everything mapped out. He was covering all of the three areas highlighted above.

Julie was giving it conscious thought, but only at the time when opportunities cropped up for her. Therefore, at any moment she was aware of how she was reacting to current circumstances. However, she was not really thinking about how she was creating her future. The programme gave her opportunity to give some conscious thinking time to her future.

Geoff really gave it no conscious thought at all. In fact Geoff, at the beginning of the programme, did not really want to take any responsibility for his career. He felt his career was nothing to do with any decisions that he had made. By participating in the programme Geoff came to realise that he had in fact unconsciously been influencing his career. He had just let things happen to him. The programme enabled him to see that he did have a choice. It gave him the chance to consider these, and other issues. He was able to consciously decide how he wanted to manage his career in the future.

12. How are you managing?

Having focused on others, now let's return to you. Take the opportunity to think about how you are currently managing your career.

PICK UP YOUR PEN

Note down your replies to the three questions below. This will allow you to measure how aware you are of the three key areas important to managing your career.

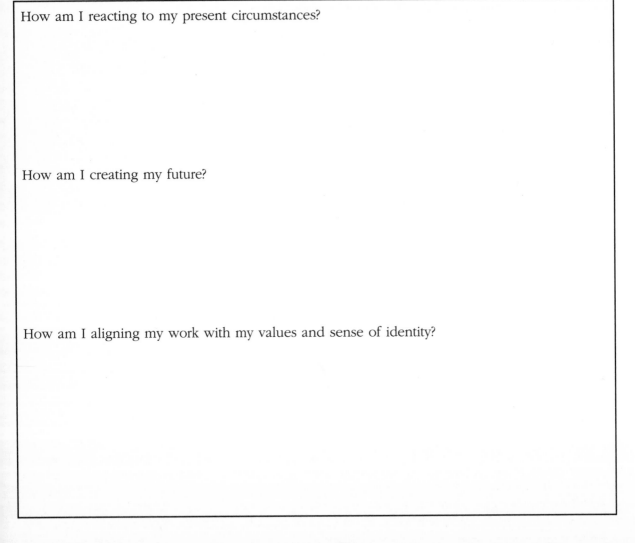

How am I reacting to my present circumstances?

How am I creating my future?

How am I aligning my work with my values and sense of identity?

If you feel that you haven't being doing much to manage your career, just by considering these three questions you are making a good start. Relax if the questions appear difficult to answer at the moment – this may be because you previously haven't given much time and thought to these areas. The information and activities in this book will help you to build on this good start, and encourage you to explore further the issues involved in going to work on your career.

If you found that your answers to the questions came easily, it is likely that you have already been spending some time contemplating your career. However, it is worth doing activities like this on a regular basis. This acts as a self-check that you have actions in place that allow you to proactively manage your career.

13.   Have a strategy

We will use Julie and William as an example one more time. Whilst working with Julie and William, to help them get what they wanted from the career programme, we moved on from looking at managing their careers, to how they were developing a strategy for managing their careers. At this point it is useful to introduce you to our definition of a career management strategy:

"A career management strategy is having a deliberate direction or purpose and being able to recognise and take advantage of opportunities as they emerge."
Go to Work on Your Career Programme

If you remember, Julie had gone from opportunity to opportunity, whereas William had a very definite plan. Using this definition we were able to help them look at how they could combine the two approaches.

For us, an effective strategy is not only about knowing what it is you are working towards, it is also about being open to opportunities that may be unknown to you at the time you determine what you want from your career. Sometimes people, when deciding the desired end result, can be constrained. By having their career steps so well planned, they can miss out on opportunities along the way. Being able to recognise and take advantage of emerging opportunities will help them reach their desired outcomes even quicker.

The other extreme is not having a clue of the likely end result – perhaps taking jobs or projects that are offered without really considering if these are in line with career goals. Something to mention at this point is that the 'deliberate direction or purpose' isn't always a specific job. It may be a field of work in which you want to be involved in or something you specifically want to achieve in your working life.

Looking at your career management strategy builds on the three areas to consider when managing your career. It helps you to decide what it is you want to create for your future. It clarifies if how you are currently reacting, includes grabbing emerging opportunities.

> **PICK UP YOUR PEN**

Take this opportunity to think about your own career management strategy by answering the following questions:

What is my deliberate direction or purpose?

What opportunities have I recognised and taken in the past few years?

14. The only way isn't up

When thinking about your direction and purpose, and the opportunities that emerge, remember that in a work context managing your career isn't always about job promotion. Quite often, when we go into organisations to facilitate career management programmes, a common complaint we hear from individuals is that opportunities do not exist because they are looking at 'dead men's (or women's) shoes'. The downsizing trend of the eighties and nineties has lead to much flatter structures within organisations. As a consequence you may need to broaden your view of what career management is about - and remember that opportunities may not always be an upward move!

"Success is a journey not a destination."
Ben Sweetland

Remember that a career path is very rarely a straight road. As well as moving forwards, at times you might go sideways, backwards, stay put or decide on a different path altogether. All are legitimate career moves if that is what you want at that time.

CAPTURE YOUR THOUGHTS

Having reached the end of this section take some time to note down your personal reflections and thoughts. Think about:

- What has struck a cord with me?
- What questions has this section raised for me?
- What remains unclear?
- What do I want to explore further?

PERSONAL THOUGHTS AND REFLECTIONS

THREE ACTIONS FOR YOU TO CONSIDER

Here are three suggested actions to encourage you to continuously Go to Work on Your Career.

1. Talk to others (friends, family, colleagues or anyone who will talk to you) about their careers. Focus on how they define their career. Compare this with how you define your career.

2. Put a date in your diary to review the activities in this chapter once you have read the whole of the book. The date you give yourself will depend on how quickly you read.

3. Carry on reading the book, considering the questions put to you, and doing the activities.

> **"The beginning is the most important part of the work."**
> **Plato**

FIND YOUR REASON WHY

Go to Wo... p...

The story of Margaret Burke

Margaret has enjoyed seven successful years working in a variety of different marketing roles for the telecommunications giant One2One. This dynamic and fast-paced environment has provided her with a stimulating mixture of challenges and projects to work on.

Margaret's present role, as Head of Brand Development and Communications at One2One, is the culmination of a career successfully managed entirely in the arena of marketing. It therefore surprised us to find out that she had actually left university as a Mathematics graduate!

Cast your mind back to the subjects you studied at school. Like most of us, we imagine you made choices based on what subjects were available to you; what subjects you enjoyed doing; and what subjects you were actually good at. Margaret chose the latter option and she discussed the reason she had made this decision with us. *"I had come from a background where I wasn't encouraged or expected to go to University. I knew from the age of sixteen that it was going to be quite hard for me to gain my family's support in my goal of getting a University education, unless that is, I got fantastic grades. Consequently I made the decision to study a subject that I was really good at, rather than the subjects I enjoyed."*

Margaret studied Mathematics based A levels, an area in which she readily excelled. At eighteen she found herself accepting a place to study Mathematics at University. Margaret recounted to us how she absolutely hated the course. *"I couldn't relate to any of the other people on the course. My friends were all doing degrees that sounded much more exciting. To try and make my situation a little better I started to study Statistics as well. However, I honestly don't know why I never contemplated fundamentally changing my course. I decided I had to just get on with it and do my best even though I hated it!"*

After talking to her friends, many of who were completing degrees in Marketing; Margaret became more and more enthralled by the concepts and glamour of the subjects they discussed. She made the decision to seek some career advice on Marketing. During her careers interview Margaret was informed, in no uncertain terms, that after completing a mathematics degree she was expected to go into accountancy or a similar career, and that, *"Mathematics graduates simply don't do marketing!"*

A turning point had been reached in Margaret's life, *"I thought to myself no way – I was already doing a degree I hated even though I excelled in this field. This time I was determined to do what I enjoyed."* In spite of the odds Margaret felt strongly about this and proceeded to make

33

ns to get what she wanted. She had realised that it was critical for her to do something she enjoyed!

The decision had been made. Rather than waiting until the end of her third year at University, Margaret began canvassing for jobs in her second year. *"I made absolutely sure I was aware of the application procedures for the large corporate companies. If companies were there on the milk rounds I made sure I was there talking to them! I found out that a couple of the big corporate companies ran courses from where they selected a majority of their graduates a year in advance. After completing an application form, writing an essay, and going through a selection interview, I managed to get myself on one of these courses."*

Margaret was successful in her quest and was offered a marketing job for a leading food manufacturer. She thoroughly enjoyed her role and quickly progressed. For each subsequent career move she made, Margaret was careful to do one thing – she questioned her reason why. *"I had learnt not to do things for the wrong reason – I was so much happier, fulfiled and successful doing something I enjoyed, rather than something I was just good at!"*

"A musician must make his music, an artist must paint, and a poet must write if he is ultimately to be at peace with himself."
Abraham Maslow

---

15.   For the right reasons

Margaret's story clearly highlights that you need to be aware of your reasons for taking actions. Actions that impact on your career. The reason you decide to do something will provide the motivation to make sure it happens. This will give you the willpower, effort and energy to ensure you make a start and keep going. In this section we will also focus on your *reason why* for wanting to manage your career.

Reflecting on Margaret's story, she perhaps felt that her original reason for studying Mathematics was wrong because she hated the subject so much. However, what is clear is that it was a strong enough reason to enable her to succeed. She really wanted to go to university and ultimately she had a good enough reason why to put up with doing something she disliked. Her desire to go to university provided enough motivation for her to continue her studies until she decided to make a change.

We have found when talking to people about their careers that there are lots of things that they will talk about doing. However, it is only when they have a strong underlying purpose that they actually take action and make it happen. We bet you'll have heard people complaining about their work, their boss, the company, the people they work with, and guess what – they've been working there for years and will probably continue to do so. They just haven't got a strong enough reason to make the change.

**"If you are to do what you want with your time,
you must learn what you don't want."**

PICK UP YOUR PEN

Let's start to examine your motivation for being where you currently are with your career. Consider, and note down, your answers to these questions:

What was the reason you moved into your current job?

What is the reason that you continue to stay in this job?

How strong is your reason for staying?

These questions are not designed to make you think you should be changing jobs; but to help you to understand the reason you are deciding to stay where you are at this point in your career; or why you might be thinking about making a change. Later in this section, and in the next two sections of the book, **DECIDE WHAT IS IMPORTANT TO YOU** (page 47) and **ACHIEVE A BALANCE** (page 65), we will give you the chance to explore the values and priorities on which your reasons are based.

**Work is what gives us purpose, identity and structure
– see it as meaningful not a drudge.**

---

16. Discover reasons for managing your career

So far we have talked about reasons for making decisions, or taking actions that have an impact on your career. We now want to relate this to reasons for managing your career. What are the reasons you have for wanting to actively manage your career? And how strong are these reasons?

It would be very easy to go through this book, get all excited about working on your career and then put it on the shelf and forget about it. To maintain the enthusiasm to manage your career it is worth establishing exactly why you might want to consciously manage your career.

PICK UP YOUR PEN

Firstly, consider this question and jot down your reply.

What was your reason for picking up and reading this book?

Your reply to this question may have highlighted the reason you are currently thinking more about managing your career. It may just be that you are reading the book out of interest or because someone passed it on to you.

Secondly, think of all the reasons you might want to focus on going to work on your career. Make a list below.

My reasons for going to work on my career are:
-
-
-
-
-
-
-
-
-
-

Thirdly, make a list of all the reasons for not going to work on your career – all the things that might stop you and get in the way.

My reasons for not going to work on my career:
-
-
-
-
-
-
-
-
-
-

Now, take some time to compare and assess the two lists. Which of your reasons are the strongest? This will show how strong your current motivation is to manage your career. If you feel it is a bit on the weak side don't give up. Reading this book will supply you with some more, or stronger, reasons for wanting to Go to Work on Your Career.

17. Give added value to your motivation

We will touch more on working with your personal values in the next section of the book, **DECIDE WHAT IS IMPORTANT TO YOU** (page 47). Nevertheless, personal values are worth mentioning at this point as they are intrinsic to your reasons and actions. When talking about values, we are describing those aspects of life we value as important. Our core values guide our everyday behaviour and the decisions we make, both at home and work.

> **PICK UP YOUR PEN**

Look back to the previous activity and the notes you have made about your reasons to Go to Work on Your Career. For each reason that you identified answer the following question:

What makes this reason important to me?
-
-
-
-
-
-
-
-
-
-

Completing this activity will have highlighted some of your personal values.

Take some time to personally assess if your reasons for going to work on your career link to those values that you feel are most important to you. If they do, you are likely to have a strong motivation to stick with managing your career. If not, it may be that you haven't yet identified a strong enough *reason why* to want to Go to Work on Your Career. So, read on.

18.   Measure your passion

We, as part of the Go MAD® team, are passionate about the work we do and the reasons we do it. Even though we all have varying personal reasons for being involved in our current work, we are all passionate about helping individuals and organisations to learn, develop and make a difference. To prove how passionate we are, rather than having a mission statement like many companies, we have a passion statement. The purpose of our passion statement is to describe how we work as a company both internally and externally.

Let us share our passion statement with you:

Being the brightness is one step beyond seeing the light. To be passionate about opening minds, encouraging development, gaining insight, exploring parameters, igniting desires, harnessing energy, inspiring people, moving forward, increasing options, stimulating ideas, creating breakthroughs, building relationships, developing skills, sowing thoughts, achieving goals, reviewing effectiveness, releasing potential, facing fears, generating happiness, taking responsibility, enjoying learning, overcoming obstacles, building teams, facilitating success, having fun, getting started, believing in choices, being the brightness and making a difference. The answers are on the inside.

So, for us the passion statement explains what we do, and encompasses what we are about. Consequently, it forms a large part of our *reason why*.

Now, we are not suggesting that you sit down and write out your own passion statement (unless you want to of course!). However, it is worth thinking about what you are passionate about, as this will impact on your reasons for choosing a particular field of work, a specific career path and whether or not to do something.

Life should be full of passion, purpose, enjoyment and courage.

PICK UP YOUR PEN

Take this opportunity to write down all the things that you are passionate about. You may also want to extend this to outside of work, as this will impact on what you choose to do while you are in work. We have given a few pointers to help you with this. Write anything down that springs to mind.

My Passions:
What am I passionate about doing?
Who am I passionate about helping or supporting?
What am I passionate about being as an individual?

Look back to page 36 where you listed your reasons for choosing your current job. See what links there are between your passions and your list of reasons. As with the previous activity, this ties in very closely with your personal values.

19.   Identify the direction you are moving in

When you have previously changed jobs, was it because you were attracted to the new job and all that it had to offer, or because it was part of your career plan? Or was it simply because you couldn't stand the job you were doing any longer and just wanted to get away from it?

**"When you get sick and tired of being
sick and tired you'll change."
Andrew Matthews**

Considering this will help you to appraise if you are motivated by moving towards a goal or moving away from a problem. Both are okay as motivators, however, it is useful to spot the difference. If you are motivated by moving away from a problem, your motivation will decrease the further you get away from the problem itself. Take the example of James, who we met when delivering a corporate career management workshop.

James was originally in a job he really enjoyed. Then he got a new boss who he couldn't stand. James wanted to move away from his boss. He successfully applied for another job in a different department within the same company. James then had a boss he liked and at first everything was great. As the memory of his previous boss faded he realised he didn't really enjoy the work he was doing. There was nothing there to keep him motivated to continue with the role. Hence, James found himself in the situation of looking for another job.

The opposite of this motivator is highlighted by Margaret's story at the beginning of the section. She was motivated towards her aims and goals: to get to university; to get on a graduate programme; and to get into Marketing.

So, if you continually move away from problems or things that are causing you dissatisfaction, as that dissatisfaction fades it can prove difficult to remain motivated. This is why it is beneficial to think about what you want from a job or career so that you are able to maintain your motivation by moving towards what it is you want.

20. Make your reason stronger

You have the choice to decide whether or not to manage your career. You can decide that you haven't got a strong enough reason why or, alternatively, you can decide you have. If you already have a strong reason then that's great. If not, you can decide to make your *reason why* stronger. We stress, at this point, that it is important for you to decide your reasons why. Working with someone else's reasons will not keep you going – it must be because it is important to you!

You can make your reason stronger by thinking about what you want, rather than focussing on getting away from something you don't want. We will help you with this when looking at defining your career goals, later in the book.

You can also make your reason stronger by consciously looking to strengthen it. If you haven't identified any strong reasons for managing your career, ask yourself what might give you a strong reason? We often find people decide they have a strong enough motive to take action on their career when their job becomes redundant or ill health threatens. Why wait? Start now and you will be more prepared for the situations you encounter.

**The greatest threat towards your future career is
your indifference to your career.**

---

21.   Remind yourself to keep going

Having identified a strong reason for managing your career, you will need to remind yourself of this reason to keep your motivation going. This is essential at those times you decide to make changes within your career. So consider, *"How can I keep reminding myself of my reasons for choosing to do this?"* This will help to maintain your motivation.

**"Motivation is when your dreams
put on work clothes."
Parkes Robinson**

Here are a few ideas of things you can do to remind yourself to keep going:

- Write down your reasons and keep them somewhere visible.
- Tell someone else what your reasons are.
- Put a date in your diary to review your reasons and check they are strong enough.
- Remind yourself how strong your reasons are by developing a statement you can review, *"My reasons are strong because ...."*

And, finally, use this book to develop your career goals and plans. These will give you an even stronger reason to carry on going to work on your career.

CAPTURE YOUR THOUGHTS

Having reached the end of this section take some time to note down your personal reflections and thoughts. Think about:

- How does Margaret's story, and her reasons for making decisions, relate to my situation?
- What have been some of my strongest *reasons why* for taking career management action?
- What issues has this section raised for me?
- What else do I need to do to strengthen my reasons for going to work on my career?

PERSONAL THOUGHTS AND REFLECTIONS

THREE ACTIONS FOR YOU TO CONSIDER

Here are three suggested actions to help you focus on using your *reasons why* to Go to Work on Your Career.

1. Write down your reasons for managing your career, and put them somewhere you can see them every day.

2. Look back over your career and identify if there is a pattern of you either being motivated towards a goal, or away from a problem. If the motive for action has usually been away from, start to think about what you might be motivated towards.

3. Decide if your *reason why* for managing your career is strong enough. If not, think of ways you can make it stronger.

DECIDE WHAT IS IMPORTANT TO YOU

The story of Sarah Armitage

After completing a degree in Social and Educational Psychology, Sarah Armitage made the decision that she wanted to become an Educational Psychologist. She found developmental psychology fascinating and felt that this would be the way forward for her.

Sarah was, however, forced to reconsider her reasons for pursuing this choice. In addition to her undergraduate degree she would also have to complete a further year's teacher training, and a minimum of two years teaching practice. *"Teaching wasn't what I wanted to do, although I knew I would have to go through this if I wanted to become an Educational Psychologist."* Despite her reservations Sarah applied for teacher training and was offered a place. *"I suddenly began to have doubts about accepting the place – did I really want to go through the pain of two years teaching? I decided that although the developmental aspects of the course appealed to me I really didn't want to apply them to teaching."* Sarah withdrew her application at this point and, because of personal commitments, ended up moving to another area of the country.

The saga didn't end there though – Sarah's story highlights the difficulties we may have making decisions we are totally comfortable with in our career development. Sarah, on a roundabout of indecision, reapplied for teacher training. Again she successfully reached the final stage of the application process and began to have serious doubts. This time Sarah withdrew her application for good. She decided to take some time out to really think about what she wanted to do – she had definitely decided by this time that she didn't want to be an Educational Psychologist that badly!

As a temporary measure, Sarah found employment in a small, family run, department store. Much to her surprise she really enjoyed her role, especially dealing with customers. Sarah describes the store as being like 'Grace Brothers', in the TV comedy 'Are You Being Served'! Those of us who are old enough will appreciate the environment Sarah was working in – the store had many loyal customers who relied on the service they delivered. *"I was given a lot of autonomy in the store and I absolutely loved it!"* Sarah's enthusiasm for working with people developed. She volunteered to manage more and more initiatives within the store and quickly gained both experience and a passion for Personnel and Human Resources.

We could leave Sarah's story there. Needless to say she continued to progress through her career in H.R. gaining both experience and qualifications along the way! Sarah is presently employed as an extremely successful Human Resources Advisor at Acordis Acetates. However, we decided it was important to share with you one more of the difficult decisions Sarah had to make early in her career…

After completing her first year qualifications with the Chartered Institute of Personnel and Development, Sarah decided it would be pertinent to move from the department store to a larger organisation, which would give her a bigger arena in which to develop. Sarah took up a place on a graduate training scheme at a well-known DIY outlet. The course lasted for eight weeks – every day of which Sarah *"hated"*. Sarah described to us how she felt that the company, and her managers, had *"dubious"* values. She felt both uncomfortable and undervalued. Nevertheless Sarah stuck out the eight weeks training, hoping that her first store placement would be a better experience and she would be able to add value to both herself and the company who had trained her.

Unfortunately for Sarah, things went from bad to worse. The manager of the store to which Sarah was allocated had the same manner as those who had administered the training programme. Sarah felt that both she and the other staff were treated appallingly. She questioned both the company's values and the professionalism of the management they employed. After just two weeks Sarah made the difficult decision to quit. Imagine, you have just completed an eight-week training course by a major organisation, you have no job to go to and you're aware that future employers may view your resignation with suspicion – how would you feel?

Sarah had realised the risks she was taking; she went on to describe to us how she felt, *"I knew I would be in a dubious position walking out on a job in this manner, but I was so unhappy. The whole thing just didn't feel right. I was compromising my own values and myself. I had learnt a valuable lesson – I knew the importance of working with people I respected."*

Once again Sarah had made a difficult decision, but she stood by her principles, left the job, and looked for another way to continue in her career. She approached an employment agency, explained her predicament, and quickly found another Human Resources role. The rest – well the rest is history!

"Some people reach the top of the ladder only to find
it is leaning against the wrong wall."
Source Unknown

---

22. Determine your values

One of the clear messages from this story is Sarah's need to ensure that her employer's values were aligned with her personal values. It was important to her to work with people that she respected. This respect was based on Sarah's observation of how they treated their employees. She felt it was important that people were treated with respect and acted with professionalism.

Before you can decide if you and your employer's values match, you need to determine what your values are. We started to consider this in the last section of the book, **FIND YOUR REASON WHY** (page 33). We described *values* as those aspects of life that we value as important. Our core values guide our everyday behaviour at home and at work. Our values will impact on our job satisfaction, as clearly demonstrated by Sarah's story. She did not feel satisfied with her job because it was misaligned with what she herself valued.

PICK UP YOUR PEN

The activity on the next page will help you reaffirm, or identify, the values you hold.

Look at the values listed in the left-hand column. Firstly, identify those that are significant to you by putting a tick in the column headed 'significant'. Then, indicate in the last column those that are most significant to you.

PERSONAL VALUES INCLUDE:	SIGNIFICANT	MOST SIGNIFICANT
ACCOMPLISHMENT – attaining goals and a sense of achievement		
AFFECTION – love, caring and fondness		
BELONGING – participating with, being involved and including others		
CHALLENGE – adventure, new and exciting experience		
COMPETIVENESS – striving to win, being the best		
CONTRIBUTION – assisting others and improving society		
CREATIVITY – being imaginative, inventive and original		
ECONOMIC SECURITY – having steady and adequate income		
FAME – being renowned, and having distinction		
FAMILY HAPPINESS – close relationship with family members		
FRIENDSHIP – close relationships with others		
HONESTY – integrity and standing up for your beliefs		
INDEPENDENCE – freedom, autonomy and liberty		
INNER HARMONY – being at peace with yourself and others		
LOYALTY – commitment, dedication and dependability		
ORDER – organised, structured and systematic		

PERSONAL DEVELOPMENT – learning and realising your potential		
PLEASURE – fun, enjoyment and good times		
POWER – influence, importance and authority		
PROGRESSION – promotion and advancement		
RECOGNITION – gaining respect and acknowledgement from others		
SELF-BELIEF – having belief in your own abilities, self-respect for who you are as an individual		
SPIRITUALITY – having faith and strong spiritual and/or religious beliefs		
TEAMWORK – collaboration and co-operation		
WEALTH – abundance and getting rich		
WELL BEING – physical and mental good health		
WISDOM – discovering knowledge, insight and enlightenment		

If you had any difficulty evaluating which are your most significant values, prioritise your values by asking yourself *"why"* that value is significant to you. If the value is important *"just because,"* as opposed to a logical explanation, you can conclude that it is important as an end in itself. However, if the answer to *"why"* leads you to another value, for example: *"Fame is important to me because it will give me more power,"* the conclusion is that 'power' is more important as a value than 'fame', as 'fame' is the means of achieving 'power'.

> **"Whosoever knows others is clever.**
> **Whosoever knows himself is wise."**
> **Lao Tzu**

We have found that a good way to check that you have correctly identified your personal values is to consider if the values you have identified are consistent with what you do on a daily basis. We have come across numerous people who say that *'health'* is their most important value. However, they continue to smoke, drink alcohol heavily and never exercise. Review the values you have chosen as your most important and look at their consistency with your everyday behaviour and the decisions that you make.

23.   Value your values

In determining your values there are two points that are essential for you to remember. Firstly, they are your values and no one else's. No values are right or wrong, and as long as they are the values that are important to you, then they are right. Recognise that others may have different values and that's okay. Only you can ultimately determine what is important to you.

Secondly, your values may alter or develop as you reach different stages in your life. With each life experience we learn, grow and change, therefore our values are also bound to change. We will also have different influences: family, friends, teachers, work colleagues and others, which will impact on the values we form and retain. If you are serious about managing your career be prepared to take some time now and again to reflect on what is currently important to you.

24.   Align your values

In his book *Go MAD® The Art of Making A Difference*, Andy Gilbert relates his own personal story describing the point he realised that his personal values were not aligned to the company he was working for:

"In November 1996, I completed the dissertation of my Masters degree in Human Resource Development. It focused on how people managed their careers – or rather didn't in the majority of cases. I realised that whilst I knew the theory of career management, and had helped many others with their careers, I was not applying it to myself. I was in a rut. A career rut. Feeling let down and trapped inside a company where the short term objectives and behaviour of the directors conflicted with my personal values. I concluded that I needed to align the work I did in the future with my values. I made the decision to leave my job and establish a values driven training and development consultancy. Six weeks later I escaped from the rut and Career Strategies Ltd was formed as a vehicle for my dreams."

What Andy discovered was his *reason why*. He found a strong enough reason for making a move and getting out of a rut. Being aware of your values will help you determine if your personal motivation is strong enough for you to take action. Use them as a self-check when making career decisions. Assess how the action you are considering, be it a new job or a new area of work, aligns with your personal values. This will give you the motivation for seeing your actions through.

"Make your work be in keeping with your purpose."
Leonardo Da Vinci

---

25.   Love the work you do

In the previous section of the book, **FIND YOUR REASON WHY** (page 33), we talked about being passionate about work. We invited you to consider what you felt passionate about. If your work aligns with your personal values you will be passionate about your work. In fact it might not even feel like work because you will love what you are doing so much.

As part of our ongoing research, Andy interviewed Rosemary Conley, the creator of the 'Hip and Thigh Diet', for the Go MAD® monthly audiotape programme. She described in detail how much she loves working with people. Her passion is to help those people who want to improve their lives by taking better care of their diet and fitness. She loves the work she does and in the process has become extremely successful. Her work is in exact alignment to her personal values and passion.

**"The miracle is not that we do this work,
but that we are happy to do it."
Mother Theresa**

ASK YOURSELF THIS

- How well do the values of my organisation match my personal values?
- How passionate do I feel about the work I do?
- What needs to happen for me to love the work I do?

26.   Determine your own success

How will you know if you are successful? This will depend upon what success means to you. What success means for you will be dependent on your core values and the strength of your reason for pursuing personal goals or a particular career path.

Quite often when asked what success means to them people say, *"being happy"*. But what does this mean? What makes one person happy will not necessarily make the next person happy. It is up to you to determine what success is for you.

Sue, who attended a career workshop with us last year, recognised she had strong core values around family happiness. She realised she was happiest when spending time with her partner, children and close family. Her job was not allowing her time to feel she was successfully achieving this. She decided she would feel greater success and happiness by cutting her working hours to enable her to devote more time to her family. This was going to impact on her progression within the company. However, knowing what success meant for her, Sue was confident and happy to make these changes.

ASK YOURSELF

- What does success mean to me?
- What makes me happy?

"We are prone to judge success by the index of our salaries or the size of our automobile rather than by the quality of service and relationship to mankind."
Martin Luther King Jnr

27.   Recognise your life priorities

To help add to your personal picture of success and build on the values already identified, it is important to reflect on the priorities in your life.

PICK UP YOUR PEN

One way of doing this is to imagine yourself in the future – perhaps aged 65 or 70. Imagine you have achieved your success as you defined it. Take yourself forward to that time and place. Now, think back over your life and, from the following list, pick those statements that reflect your success.

- I was in the top 3% of my profession.
- I've made a lot of money from my work.
- I spent a lot of time with my children helping them to learn and develop.
- I own a superb car and house.
- I rose to the top in my organisation.
- I had some wonderful and exotic holidays.
- My best times were and are spent with my family.
- I have learned something new every week.
- I considered my partner's needs at all times and worked hard to ensure a loving relationship.
- I have taken good care of my health.
- I have creative pastimes such as painting or playing a musical instrument.
- I travelled the world having fantastic experiences along the way.
- I made a contribution to the world.
- I have built long-lasting friendships and worked to maintain these friendships.
- I am kind and caring to others.
- I had lots of challenges and adventures.
- I live each day to the full.
- I have made a difference to the world.

ASK YOURSELF

- What else (if anything) would I add to the list as a priority?
- How well does this match the way I live my life at the moment?
- How do my life priorities match with the personal values I identified previously?

28. Build your picture of what is important to you

So far we have focused on your personal values, how well the work you do is aligned to your personal values, what your life priorities might be and whether you have a strong enough reason to take action. To continue to build a picture of what is important to you, we will now tune into the factors that you need to have present in the workplace – the factors that will add to your job satisfaction. It is highly probable that these factors will link closely to your personal values.

Let's look back to Sarah's story at the beginning of this section. The factors important to Sarah in the workplace were autonomy and the opportunity to manage human resource issues. These are linked with her strong personal values of being treated, and treating others, with respect.

"Everyone has been made for some particular work, and the desire for that has been put in every heart."
Rumi

As well as your personal values influencing future career decisions, it is also useful to think about the key factors you want to be present in the workplace. When weighing up any job, or project offers, you can then check whether these factors will be in place for you.

PICK UP YOUR PEN

Take some time to reflect on the 18 factors described overleaf. Pick five that you feel are essential for you in the workplace. We ask you to pick only five so that you think of the factors that are most important to you – it would be easy to say that all of them are important. There are no right or wrong answers – it's entirely a personal matter.

SECURITY	LOW PRESSURE	TEAM WORK
A job for life: a long-term career path with reasonable financial reward.	A job that is mainly predictable in which others set the objectives and direction. No time pressures, and workloads that are consistently manageable within the working hours agreed.	Working as part of a team and feeling part of the team. Frequent contact with others and the chance to develop personal relationships. Friendly and sociable environment.
PROMOTION	**WORKING CONDITIONS**	**VARIETY**
A job that provides the opportunity to get ahead quickly and move up the career ladder.	A workplace that is pleasant, well designed, clean and tidy.	Ongoing changes and plenty of opportunity for personal development and new learning.
CONTRIBUTION	**EXCITEMENT**	**LEADING OTHERS**
The chance to directly impact on the success of the organisation. Making a lasting contribution.	Risk taking, a job that provides the opportunity for adventure and demands the best use of abilities and qualities.	The power to decide direction and to direct others. Accountability, the authority for important tasks, and the opportunity to influence others.

ENTREPRENEURSHIP	INNOVATION	STATUS
The desire to be self-employed, to develop new products and services. The definition of self to be through work and profit or gain.	The opportunity to produce new ideas and be creative. To be able to create new products, services and spend time problem solving.	To be in a job others view as important. To be looked up to in a particular area of work. To be a recognised expert.
INCOME	**LIFE BALANCE**	**PROCEDURES DRIVEN**
To have high earnings. Money to spend on the extras. To lead a prosperous lifestyle.	Work that allows a balance of life. Leaving time for friends, family and leisure pursuits.	Work where strict procedures are laid down. There is a 'right way' of doing things and instructions to follow.
SELF-MOTIVATED	**LOCATION**	**HIGH PRESSURE**
To be independent in making decisions about managing workloads and priorities. To be self-reliant.	Location of work is of extreme importance. A location that matches lifestyle or the community you want to be involved in.	High pace, competitive important work, working to tight deadlines. Heavy workload and problem solving as a key area of the job.

- How do the factors I have picked as the most important link to my personal values?
- How many of the desired factors are present for me in my current job?
- Are there any other factors that I can add?

29. Go for job satisfaction

Having a job gives people purpose and a sense of identity. Quite often when asked about themselves, the first thing people say is their job title – *"doctor," "training consultant," "shop assistant," "team leader"* and so on. Throughout this section we have been considering issues that hopefully encourage you to reflect on whether your job reflects your purpose and the sense of identity that you want. That your job satisfies the things that are important to you. If it does, you have more of a chance of feeling job satisfaction and even enjoying your work!

Job satisfaction is about having the following aspects in place: work that matches your personal values, work that you feel motivated to do, and work that meets all the factors that are important to you in the workplace. Every day at work might not go exactly as you want, but wouldn't it be great to look forward to Monday instead of wishing it was Friday?

Here are two examples of people we have met who realised that their work didn't give them the purpose or job satisfaction that they required. Having realised it, they decided to do something about it.

We interviewed Nick a few years ago as part of the initial Making A Difference research. Nick had been working in the City and earning vast amounts of money, just as his father had before him. Nick came to a realisation that he didn't enjoy the work or the lifestyle that went with it – it wasn't the sense of identity he wanted. He gave it all up.

He became a priest – obviously not overnight – and went to work in an economically deprived area of Liverpool. At the time we spoke to him, Nick had achieved what he wanted – a job where he felt he had a purpose, a purpose that was closely aligned to his personal values.

Kathryn uses the example of an ex-colleague Dawn. Dawn had a job that was okay, nothing thrilling but she didn't particularly hate it. Dawn decided she wanted to do something that gave her more job satisfaction. Having thought about it she decided she wanted to teach, and teach a subject she had a personal interest in – History. Sounds easy doesn't it? Dawn definitely proved that her reason why was strong enough! She had to take her A levels, then do a degree, then teacher training, all as a single parent with two children. Five years later she achieved her goal. Dawn has now been a teacher for three years and she loves her job. She has achieved what she wanted – fantastic job satisfaction!

For both of these people, the changes they made were not easy. However, for them it was worth it! They obtained what was important for them. These examples give a clear message; if you are not satisfied in your job, do something – go for satisfaction. You don't have to take such extreme actions as described in these examples, i.e. complete changes of career direction. However, adding one of the factors that give you job satisfaction will start to make a difference and encourage you to take further action. A number of small differences added together can make a big difference.

Why not enjoy the time you spend at work as much as the time you spend out of it?

If you currently have job satisfaction, think about how you can ensure it continues. What specifically is in place that helps you to achieve job satisfaction and how can you ensure it remains?

CAPTURE YOUR THOUGHTS

Having reached the end of this section take some time to review the issues raised, noting down your personal thoughts and reflections. Consider:

- What are my personal values?
- What are the values of my organisation and how do these align with my personal values?
- What gives me greatest job satisfaction?
- In what areas would I like my job satisfaction to be increased?
- What sense of purpose and identity do I want to have?
- What would be the perfect job, to match exactly all the things that are important to me?

PERSONAL THOUGHTS AND REFLECTIONS

THREE ACTIONS FOR YOU TO CONSIDER

Here are three suggested actions to help you continue to determine what is important to you.

1. Write a description of the job that would encompass all the factors you have identified as being important to you. How does this compare with your current job?

2. If you are in a long-term relationship, ask your partner to complete the life priorities activity. Take some time to discuss what is important to both of you and how your personal priorities impact on each other.

3. Consider how your personal values have been formed. What and who has influenced you? What is likely to influence you in the future? How will this impact on your career?

"My formula for living is quite simple. I get up in the morning and I go to bed at night. In between, I occupy myself as best I can."
Cary Grant

ACHIEVE A BALANCE

The story of Carl Robley

What do you base your career decisions on? Carl, an Area Manager for One2One, has achieved what some people believe to be impossible – a career balanced successfully with his priorities in life.

Carl left home at the age of sixteen to attend Fleetwood Nautical College and train to be a Radio Operator with the Merchant Navy. Unlike school, where he was always told he had the ability to succeed but lacked the motivation, Carl excelled in his studies. *"I found out that once I liked something I was good at it."* From an intake of twenty-four, Carl was one of only four who successfully completed the required three-year college programme. When we asked Carl why he thought he'd been successful he described how he had taken full advantage of what was available to him. *"The college offered us plenty of extra support. For example, we could take past papers home to study and the tutors would be happy to mark them for us. Unlike most of my peers I was sixteen and living away from home. I managed on little money, and couldn't even legally go to the pub for a drink – so I studied. This was no hardship to me. I enjoyed the subject and I had nothing better to do!"*

Owing to his pragmatic nature Carl left college a fully qualified Radio Operator. Following his graduation he was anxious to gain a posting at sea, however, there was one more course he would have to complete as a pre-requisite for seafaring employment.

At this point in time, the Merchant Navy was in decline and Carl knew that there was a chance he would have to take a shore based posting. However, he decided he was going to do everything in his power to get a job aboard ship. Once again Carl considered his circumstances. While completing the three-month course, which would allow him to go to sea, Carl took steps to market himself. *"I visited my local library and got hold of a copy of the 'Lloyd's Register of British Shipping'. I wrote to every ship owner who had more than two vessels. I explained my position and asked if there were any vacancies. There must have been over two hundred letters. It cost me a small fortune in stamps!"*

By this time Carl had moved back home, and after completing the three-month postgraduate course he was left with a dilemma. *"I couldn't go to sea because the results from my exams took three months to come through. Like my peers I was left with a choice. Sit around for three months and wait, sign on for benefits and claim unemployment – or do something constructive!"* You guessed it – Carl chose the latter option. With the help and support of the

Local Education Authority and his parents, he completed three more courses he felt would give him an edge in his search for sea-going employment.

His proactivity paid off, as a result of the 200 letters and his insatiable appetite for learning, Carl was offered not one, but several jobs on board ship. During the next few years he continued to progress through distance learning while at sea, and completed short courses while on shore leave.

After six successful years, Carl's career in the Navy drew to a close. Despite the availability of shore postings he found that he was still required to work at sea. Carl described how his career simply wasn't compatible with what he now wanted from life. His priorities had changed; he had a wife and young baby and wanted to spend more time with them.

A decision was made and Carl began to look outside the Navy for suitable jobs. After showing the same tenacity he had displayed while looking for sea-faring employment, Carl quickly identified several roles that grabbed his interest. One of which was as a Field Support Technician at One2One.

Following his successful application, Carl was quick to let his managers know of his drive and ambition. After commuting for a while, an opportunity arose for Carl to work closer to home. If Carl accepted the position he would be required to spend far less time commuting to and from work. However, he was also aware it would mean a move away from the Head Office of One2One. Carl described that he felt the move could possibly become career limiting. However, when he weighed this against the benefits he would gain in his home life the decision became much easier to make.

He decided to make the move closer to home. Carl was then able to focus on both his career and growing family in equal measures. In fact his relocation has proved to be far from career limiting. His proactive and determined nature, combined with One2One's support and facilitation, have resulted in a comfortable balance for Carl between work and his life.

"It's not how many hours you put in, but how much you put into those hours."
Source Unknown

---

30. Find the balance

Carl's story highlights many vital points that need to be considered when managing a career, namely taking responsibility to personally develop, being proactive, and making the most of opportunities. These points are covered in later sections of the book. In this section we focus specifically on achieving work life balance. For ease, we will call it life balance.

So what is life balance? It's about finding the balance you want in your life. Determining how much time you want to spend at work and what you want to do with your time out of work. Carl wanted to achieve a balance, which enabled him to spend time with his family. You will need to determine what is the right balance for you.

31. Be a balancing act

Your values and priorities (as identified earlier in the book) will help you to determine the right life balance. Like Carl, this may be about having time with family and friends. For some people this might be putting more time and effort into their working life. For others it may be focusing on health and fitness. For some it could be how they contribute to society and the world.

The balancing act is getting the elements, important to you, in place, in the right amounts, at the right time, and in the right proportions to one another. This doesn't mean allocating equal time to each area of your life; this means deciding what feels right for you – what's in line with your values and priorities. You will then be able to determine what the right balance is for you.

**Life is for living.
How do you live yours?**

PICK UP YOUR PEN

This activity will help you to explore whether you are achieving the balance you want in your life at the moment.

Start to reflect on, and identify, the areas of your life you want to include in your balancing act. You may wish to refer back to the activities in the last section of the book, **DECIDE WHAT IS IMPORTANT TO YOU** (page 47). These areas can be anything that is important to you. Some of the areas you might want to consider are:

- Work/Career
- Family (you might want to split this to consider specific individuals or groups within your family)
- Friends
- Health
- Leisure
- Spiritual well being
- Hobbies and interests
- Personal time (how much time you want to have for yourself)
- Contribution (what you give to others/society)
- Personal development (what you want to learn)
- Anything else that is important to you in your life

Now, imagine the circle on the opposite page is your life. Draw in lines (like cutting a cake or a pie) to represent how your life is **currently** divided into the areas with which you wish to achieve a balance. That is, as it is **now**.

The whole circle represents 100%. How is that 100% split? It might help if you focus on a certain period of time. Calculate how much time you give to each area over that period. The bigger the portion, the more of your time you spend in it.

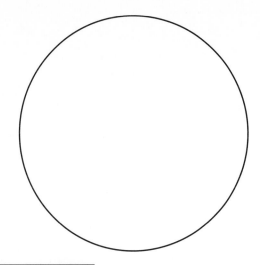

- Is this the balance I want in my life?
- How do the various slices of the pie interconnect and impact on each other?
- What would I like to be different?

**"We don't regret the things we do –
we regret the things we forget to do."
Source Unknown**

---

32.   Get the right balance

If you are happy with how your life is balanced – great! If not, consider the balance you want.

PICK UP YOUR PEN

Use the circle on the following page to represent your life. This time draw in the portions of your life not as they are now, but how you would **like** them to be.

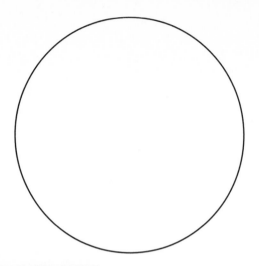

ASK YOURSELF

- What needs to happen for me to achieve this balance in my life?
- What do I need others to do?
- What do I need to do?

33. Measure the quality

Achieving a balanced life isn't just about the amount of time spent in each area of your life. Your life balance will also be affected by what you do in that time. For example, someone might identify that they want to place more emphasis on family relationships. Hence, they decide to leave work earlier three times a week, giving themselves more time at home. So, they go home, sit down and watch television – and then wonder why their family relationships are not improving. An additional aspect, therefore, will be determining what you want to achieve by having your balance of life. What will you achieve with that time? What will you enjoy spending your time doing?

**"Be absolutely determined to enjoy what you do."
Gerry Sikorski**

---

34.   Act like you mean it

Having decided the balance of life you want, the next step is to act like you mean it. If you want to make better use of your time outside of work, diarise what you are going to do. If you want better quality leisure time, or more time with the family, book holiday dates as a priority. If you want to progress within your organisation, set goals and write out an action plan (there will be opportunity to do this later in the book, if you haven't done it yet).

"The bitterest tears shed over graves are for words left unsaid and deeds left undone."
Source Unknown

People often talk about what they want, but then do nothing to get it. Changing how things are now, will involve taking some action. This doesn't necessarily have to be a mammoth task. Sometimes taking the simplest action can bring good results.   Here's an example of this:

We first met Tracey a few years ago on a Go to Work on Your Career workshop. Tracey loved her job in Personnel but due to workloads she was working increasingly long hours. She wanted to be able to keep ahead of her work, but also devote time to other things in her life such as fitness. Tracey left the workshop having identified steps to take in order to achieve more of a life balance.

Kathryn met Tracey a few months following the workshop. She was still working late on some days, however they were the days she had diarised. Knowing when she was going to work late, also meant Tracey could book in the other things she wanted to do. She had taken control of the situation and was determining the balance in her life.

35. Be realistic

We have already referred to managing this area of your life as a balancing act. At times you will need to juggle the various areas you have identified. Things will not always go according to plan. Be realistic about what is achievable. If you miss going to the gym because something urgent crops up at work don't give yourself a hard time – ensure it's a one off. Watch out for patterns emerging and the balance tilting too far away from what you want. Regularly review how your life is balanced. Think about this and plan to make any necessary adjustments.

36. Manage the pressure

Sometimes, in an effort to manage the balance of our life and juggle our many priorities, we can feel increasingly under pressure. Whether we describe this as pressure or stress, too much of it can affect our quality of life. So managing pressure is part and parcel of the balancing act.

"I finally figured out the only reason to be alive is to enjoy it."
Rita Mae Brown

The strange thing about pressure is that events or situations that may cause one person to feel under excessive pressure may not affect another. Therefore, it is very much an individual thing. Because of this personal interpretation, individuals must find their own methods of coping with pressure.

The good news is that we all need some pressure to exist. Paul McGee, the author of the Go MAD® book *59 Minutes to a Calmer Life,* describes it in this way:

"Is pressure a bad thing? Absolutely not. Without pressure or stimulation, life would quickly become boring and

unfulfilling. Depression and anxiety would be experienced by far more people than it is now. We need a certain amount of pressure, or a sense of challenge, to get us out of bed in the morning. As human beings, we function at our best when we have opportunities to grow and develop, and not when stuck in a comfort zone that ultimately becomes a rut. A 'stress free' or 'pressure free' life becomes a meaningless life."

So, balancing your life may bring some pressure. Hopefully, it will be stimulating pressure that you experience as you achieve the balance you desire.

ASK YOURSELF

- What causes me excessive pressure?
- What can I do to tackle the causes of pressure?
- What stimulating pressure do I have in my life?

37. Take control of your pressure

Research has shown that a feeling of lack of control is one of the main causes of stress. Managing your career and achieving life balance puts you firmly in control.

"Whatever doesn't kill you makes you strong."
Goethe

We said earlier in this section that the feelings arising from pressure are a personal thing. You can decide to tackle the causes of excessive pressure or discover what coping strategies work best for you. The main thing is to decide to take control of how you manage and cope with pressure.

PICK UP YOUR PEN

You may already have your own ways of coping with excessive pressure. If you are looking for further ways of managing pressure, listed below are 41 ideas. The book *59 Minutes to a Calmer Life* will give you even more information. Read through the list and highlight the ideas that appeal to you.

- talk to someone
- count to ten
- relaxation exercises
- scream and shout (in a room by yourself)
- hit something (preferably something soft like a pillow)
- go for a walk
- explore using massage, reflexology or other therapies
- enjoy some physical exercise
- listen to music
- do something you enjoy and that you feel totally immersed in
- focus on small steps rather than the whole task
- breathe slowly and calmly
- tell a joke
- follow a healthy diet
- be pleasant to others
- ask for help in prioritising – both in and out of work
- write down how you are feeling
- keep a journal – write down all the positive things that have happened each day
- recognise what you can't change
- say 'no' to unreasonable requests
- focus on one thing at a time
- have personal goals and priorities
- set yourself achievable goals
- put things into perspective – what's the worst that could happen?
- imagine you feel calm
- visualise a place where you feel relaxed
- avoid the people who increase your pressure levels

- read a positive book that makes you feel good
- prioritise and organise your work and life
- enjoy the present and worry less about the future
- be realistic – sometimes things will not go according to plan but you can cope
- recognise how your reaction affects the situation
- celebrate your successes
- slow down – walking, eating, talking, driving
- ask for help
- take a break
- put in 100% effort – this gets things done quicker
- be prepared for those situations in which you know you will feel pressurised
- worry less about what people think of you
- aim to be less than perfect – a good job will be good enough
- **above all, work out what works for you**

ASK YOURSELF

- Which of these ideas appeal to me most?
- What else would I add to this list to help me manage pressure?
- What can I start doing today that will reduce unnecessary pressure in my life?

**"We don't stop playing because we grow old,
we grow old because we stop playing."
Source Unknown**

---

38. Have a cut-off point

Sometimes it can be useful to have a cut-off point between work and home. This will stop you taking work pressures home. It will also stop you taking home pressures to work. Therefore, you will be more relaxed and focused both at work and at home. It allows you to keep the balance by stopping the pressures in one area spilling over into other areas of your life.

If you walk, or drive, to and from work, choose a building or a lamp post as your cut off point, or it could be a particular road or point in the pavement. If you travel by train you could choose a particular station. Your cut off point acts as a trigger; a trigger to leave work at work; a trigger to start focusing on home; a trigger to leave home worries behind; a trigger to start focusing on the day ahead at work.

ASK YOURSELF

- What could be my cut off point?

39. Keep the balance

As with most things, the life balance you want is likely to change. Your priorities will change as you move into different life stages. Watch out for the signal that things aren't quite right. It could be a feeling of excessive pressure or a wish that you had more time for some area of your life.

At these times, take a break. Give yourself some time out. Stop and think about your whole life, and the balance you want to achieve. Above all take action to get the right balance for you, at that time.

"Life isn't a matter of milestones, but of moments."
Rose Kennedy

CAPTURE YOUR THOUGHTS

Now you have reached the end of this section, allow yourself some time to reflect on the issues raised. Note down your personal thoughts and reflections. Ask yourself:

- How is my life balanced at the moment?
- How closely does this match the balance I want to achieve?
- What needs to happen for me to feel that I have achieved this balance?
- What strategies do I have for coping with pressure?

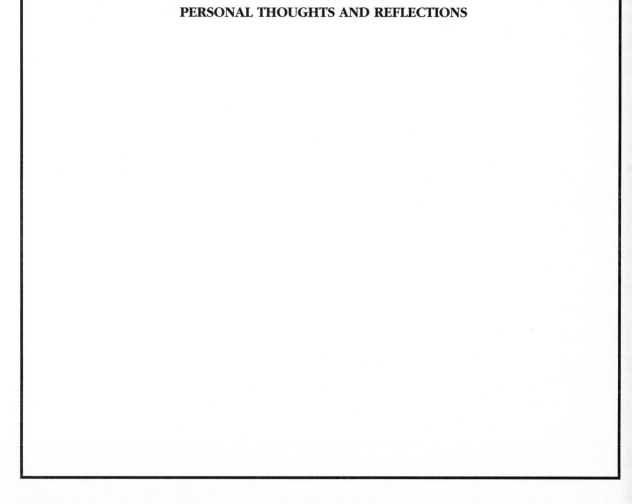

PERSONAL THOUGHTS AND REFLECTIONS

THREE ACTIONS FOR YOU TO CONSIDER

Here are three suggested actions to help you balance your life.

1. Talk to people close to you about the balance they want in their life. How does this fit with what you want? Discuss how their needs impact on the life balance you want.

2. Pick three actions from the managing pressure ideas list (page 74 and 75). Take these actions at least once over the next week. Reinforce these actions as a habit, by doing them over and over again.

3. Put a date in your diary for the next time you will review your life balance.

CONTRIBUTION FROM ONE2ONE

The Work Life Balance

One way to ensure that employees feel happy, committed and well motivated is to treat them fairly and help them to achieve an acceptable balance between their personal and professional lives. This can be done by looking at how they combine their different roles in life, and investigating whether an alternative approach will help them to achieve the work life balance they desire.

There are other more tangible reasons for considering flexible working. Firstly, and perhaps most importantly of all, the UK population is becoming older. By 2006 the 35-44 age group will be the largest age group in the working population. By 2016 this will be the 45–54 age group. Secondly, by December 2006, legislation will be introduced in the UK that outlaws age discrimination. This change in legislation will ensure that more people will return to work after taking breaks, eldercare will become as significant as childcare and less 'new entrants' will join the labour market.

We should also consider the increasingly competitive markets that most companies now operate in – not only for their customers, but also their employees. Companies need to attract and retain skilled staff, exhibit greater cost efficiency and meet customer demands for greater flexibility.

How do companies balance all these demands and still manage to remain profitable, meet their budgets and be competitive? And how will they continue to do this in the future?

Not surprisingly, one option is to introduce flexible work patterns for all staff. This is exactly what One2One has done. We recognise that the next few years will present a host of challenges for the business. We need to have a motivated and committed workforce. We understand that by helping employees balance their home and work demands both parties will gain. One2One will benefit from the retention of key staff and the skills they offer, leading to decreased staff turnover and absenteeism rates. Our employees will experience a less stressful lifestyle. They will have more freedom to pursue outside interests and responsibilities. We believe that this flexible and creative facilitation will ensure our employees benefit from their working lives.

Over the next few years, the company will look to educate, communicate, introduce and encourage options such as Compressed Hours (working 10 days hours in, for example, only 9 days), Job Sharing, Term Time Working, Home Working, Sabbaticals and Career Breaks.

The aim will be to ensure that not only are we prepared for the business environment of the future, but we also have a work culture and environment that employees enjoy being in. One that promotes a work life balance that is comfortable to all concerned.

Contributed by Steve Peace, Employee Relations Advisor

"IF I HAD MY LIFE TO LIVE OVER AGAIN"

"I'd dare to make more mistakes next time. I wouldn't be so perfect
I'd relax more, I would limber up.
I would be sillier than I have been this trip. I would take fewer things seriously.
I would take more chances, I would take more trips.
I would climb more mountains and swim more rivers.
I would eat more ice cream and fewer beans.
I would perhaps have more actual troubles but I'd have fewer imaginary ones.

You see, I'm one of those people who lives sensibly and sanely hour after hour, day after day.
Oh, I've had my moments and if I had to do it all over again, I'd have more of them.
In fact, I'd try to have nothing else. Just moments, one after another, instead of living so many years ahead of each day.
I've been one of those people who never goes anywhere without a thermometer, a hot water bottle, a raincoat and a parachute.
If I had to do it again, I would travel lighter than I have.

If I had my life to live over, I would start barefoot earlier in the spring and stay that way later in the fall.
I'd go to more dances, I'd ride more merry-go-rounds, I'd watch more sunrises and I'd play with more children, if I had my life to live over again.
But you see, I don't."

Nadine Stair (aged 85)

DEFINE YOUR GOALS

The story of Helen Bunbury

Helen Bunbury is a great believer in goal setting. As soon as she completed her graduate programme at Royal and SunAlliance, Helen set, what she believed to be, a realistic goal. After spending time researching the company structure as a whole, and observing her colleagues in their work, Helen took some time to consider the areas she could offer the most value in her performance at work.

With all this in mind, Helen set herself a goal, *"I looked at the situation and added something realistic to aim for, something to stretch myself for and something extra! Just because that's me – I like to really push myself. I developed a five year plan – I knew exactly what I wanted to achieve by the time I was twenty seven."*

Before we find out exactly what Helen's goal was, let me tell you her friends doubted her realism and questioned her sanity when she shared her objectives with them! Helen had decided that she wanted to be a Board appointed Manager within five years! Now the reasons her friends exclaimed with such horror, was because the average time it took to reach this type of appointment was between ten and fifteen years. The earliest anybody had achieved it - seven years!

Helen shared with us a secret. She argued that, *"You have to know what you want to achieve from life. If things don't go your way, don't feel sorry for yourself. Simply regroup and reassess your situation – then take a very determined view about what is going to happen."*

You see, Helen believed that the goal of reaching the position of Board appointed Manager within five years was perfectly realistic. She was also aware that the road to success would not be a smooth one – she was prepared to make adjustments to her goals and accommodate situations that arose. *"It was never about whether I would achieve a goal or not – it was always about how I was going to achieve it."*

Helen employed several measures to ensure she maintained the momentum she desired on her chosen career path. For example, she consistently approached her managers looking for a new challenge; she accepted more challenging roles – occasionally without a pay rise or grade change – simply because she felt the experience would add value to herself and bring her one step closer to her goal. In each new role, Helen identified an individual whom she felt could take over her position when she felt ready to move on. She helped to guide and support them in their development plans. Helen told us, *"I was there for the long haul, not just short term gains. I always did something that I would be interested in and that would be of value to myself as well as the company."*

Needless to say Helen achieved her goal. After many different roles, some sideways career moves and upward promotions, Helen is now a Regional Corporate Business Manager. She maintained her self-belief throughout and has enjoyed what she describes as a, *"fantastic"* career so far.

**"When you reach for the stars you may not get one,
but you won't come up with a
handful of mud either."**
Readers Digest

---

40. Decide to make a decision about what you want

Helen was very clear about what she wanted. She had a specific goal, *"To be a Board appointed Manager within five years"*. It is commonly stated that unfortunately only 3-5% of people bother to set personal goals. Why do we say unfortunately? Because the very act of defining, writing and reviewing personal goals gives your career direction and focus. And so few people do it!

**"Our plans miscarry because they have no aim.
When a person does not know what harbour he is
making for, no wind is the right wind."**
Seneca

Most employees will have some sort of goals or objectives agreed regarding their work performance. This is because employers understand that objectives help employees to keep the organisational goals in sight, understand priorities and know what is expected. Wouldn't it be good to know where you were heading, be focused on what is important to you and know what you expect of yourself? By the end of this section we will have explored these key issues in relation to your personal goal setting.

41. Identify areas for goal setting

Both work and non-work related goals will impact on your career. This may be though the work you choose to do or how you achieve balance in other areas of your life.

PICK UP YOUR PEN

To help you determine the type of goals you may want to set, consider the following questions. To answer some of the questions you will need to refer back to earlier sections of the book – these are noted for you.

If you already have personal goals, use this as an opportunity to review them. Jot down any thoughts and answers to the questions in the spaces provided.

What have you identified as your core values?
(DECIDE WHAT IS IMPORTANT TO YOU – page 50)

What are you doing to live up to your core values?

What have you identified as your life priorities?
(DECIDE WHAT IS IMPORTANT TO YOU – page 55)

What will you need to do to fulfil your life priorities?

What is your reason for being in your current job?
(**FIND YOUR REASON WHY** – page 36)

What is the balance you want to achieve in your life?
(**ACHIEVE A BALANCE** – page 69)

What things do you want to do at work or in your personal life?

What material things do you want to possess?

What do you want to learn?

What skills do you want to develop?

What experience do you want to gain?

How would you like to increase your effectiveness?

What do you want to achieve at work?

What do you want to achieve in your personal life?

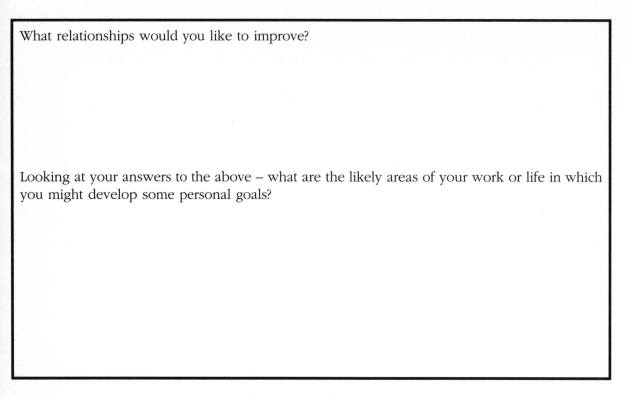

What relationships would you like to improve?

Looking at your answers to the above – what are the likely areas of your work or life in which you might develop some personal goals?

If you completed this activity you will have started to identify the types of personal goals that feel right for you. If you didn't complete this activity then you have missed an opportunity to feel more satisfied at work. Based on your values and priorities, personal goals will give you a sense of purpose. You will know why you are doing something, because you will know where you are going.

"This one step – choosing a goal and sticking to it – changes everything."
Scott Reed

---

42. Explore your reason why

For every goal you set, it is essential to determine the *reason why*. What is your motivation for wanting something as a goal? What is the motivation that will keep you focused on achieving that goal? Your motivation may link back to a core value, your life priorities or life balance. Is the reason strong enough to keep you going? We highlighted earlier in the book, that it needs to be **your reason why** – not someone else's.

"The pursuit of happiness is a most ridiculous phrase. If you pursue happiness you'll never find it."
C.P. Snow

Let us give you an example. Last year Marian attended a Go to Work on Your Career programme. She had a dilemma. Her boss wanted her to agree to the goal of becoming a Board Member within the following 12 months. Although Marian had worked hard to get to her position in the company, her life outside work was of equal importance to her. She knew if she took this position, it would impact on her balance of life. She decided that her reasons for maintaining her life balance were stronger than her reasons for becoming a Board Member. She decided to discuss other options that would have less impact on her personal life.

43.   Aspire to achieve

You could say: *"What's the point in having personal goals? You don't know whether you can achieve them or not because circumstances change. It might not be possible."* Well, you might not fully achieve your goals. But knowing the direction you are heading will definitely get you part of the way there. That's got to be better than not moving forward at all!

"Far away there in the sunshine are my highest aspirations. I may not reach them, but I can look up and see their beauty, believe in them and follow them."
Louisa May Alcott

We mentioned earlier in the book Andy's experience of interviewing Rosemary Conley, the founder of the Hip and Thigh Diet. Rosemary talked about when she was a Tupperware agent over 30 years ago. She discovered that if she hit a certain target in sales she would be rewarded with a dishwasher (not owned by many households in those days). She described how that spurred her on. It became her goal. Now she didn't know if her goal was achievable or not. But she knew if she didn't get the dishwasher she would probably have enough sales to get the automatic washing machine (again a rare commodity at that time). She also knew that had to be better than achieving enough sales for the thermos flask! She aspired to achieve.

ASK YOURSELF

- If I could achieve anything I wanted to what would it be?
- What else would I achieve in aspiring to this goal?

44.   Ignore the "Yes Buts"

People are sometimes put off goal setting by focusing too much on *how* they will achieve their goals, as opposed to identifying first *what* it is they want to achieve. They get into a long list of *"yes, but"*. Imagine someone having this conversation with themselves:

"I'd really like to earn more money. Yes, but I haven't got the qualifications to get promotion in this company. I could look elsewhere. Yes, but how do I go about getting another job? I could ask my boss for a pay rise. Yes, but he's bound to say no ...." and so on and so on.

So what they do is stop themselves from setting any goals to increase their income. Because they let the *yes, buts* get in the way. If they set the goal and then decided how they were going to achieve it, they are likely to be more definite about the actions to take.

For goal setting to be effective you need to consider the *why* and the *what* before the *how*. *What* exactly do you want to achieve? What is your *reason why* for wanting to achieve this goal? Then you can explore the *how* – all the possible actions that will help you achieve your goal.

Remember there will be some opportunities out there that you don't yet know about. If you don't know the *what,* you won't know whether they are the right opportunities for you. These opportunities will be some of the unknown *how,* just waiting to happen.

Question - "Would you tell me, please, which way I ought to go from here?"
Answer - "That depends a good deal on where you want to get to."
Alice in Wonderland

---

45.   Enjoy the journey

Determining your personal goals is not just about the end result. It is also important that you enjoy the path to their achievement. What's the point of having an end goal of becoming Managing Director if you hate all the jobs on the way there? – a possible ten years of misery! Now you might decide that the end result is worth it. That's your judgement call.

"Keep your face to the sunshine and you will never see the shadows."
Helen Keller

However, achievement of the end goal doesn't need to be the only measure of success. There may well be stages of achievement on way to the end goal. A measure of success could also be the enjoyment of the journey. In the earlier section, **DECIDE WHAT IS IMPORTANT TO YOU** (page

47), we focused on how people often define success as 'being happy'. You will need to define what will bring you happiness in your journey towards your goals.

If you don't have personal goals, how do you know if where you are heading will bring happiness? So, the goals and the journey go hand in hand – linked with your personal happiness.

"A sailor without a destination cannot hope for a favourable wind."
Leon Tec

---

46. What to do when you don't know what to do

In our career management work we sometimes meet individuals who say, *"I can't set goals, I haven't got a clue what I want to do."* In response, we make some of the following suggestions to help them move from this stage into goal setting:

1. Start small – what would you like to achieve in the next three months – six months – twelve months?
2. Imagine that you know what you want. What would it be?
3. If you were free to follow your dreams – what would you do?
4. Imagine you are a child – what do you want to do when you grow up?
5. Examine your core values and life priorities. What do they point you towards?
6. Set a goal about when you will have decided what you want. Give yourself a specific deadline.

What to do when you don't know what to do – enjoy finding out.

PICK UP YOUR PEN

This activity is only relevant if you are unsure of what you want, i.e. unsure of what your personal goals may be.

Pick two of the suggestions from the previous list and act on them. Use the space below to write your answers and thoughts.

MY THOUGHTS AND IDEAS

---

47.   Put your goals in writing

Once you have decided on your goals it is vital that you write them down. Writing goals shows you are serious about achieving them. There have been a number of research studies that have proved that the act of writing goals, as opposed to thinking them, greatly increases the likelihood of achievement. It helps you focus specifically on what you want. Plus it helps you remember them!

As well as just writing goals down, we need to consider the way they are written. With a well-written goal there is no ambiguity as to what it means. The majority of the organisations we work with use the acronym SMART when writing personal or performance goals.

Specific — a clear detailed description of what is to be accomplished.

Measurable — the goal states clearly what is to be achieved in terms of quantity, quality, time or cost.

Achievable — you have to believe that the goal is within your grasp.

Relevant — the goal is congruent with organisational goals or your personal values, priorities and should be related to a strong reason why.

Timescales — there is a clear date by when the goal is to be achieved.

Using SMART will ensure that you have a well-defined goal. A goal that gives you clear direction and clarity. Here are three examples of SMART goals written by participants on the Go to Work on Your Career programmes:

- To be Area Business Manager by my 35th birthday.

- By 31st May I will be undertaking 3 fitness activities of over 30 minutes duration each week.

- By 30th August I will have passed with distinction my Masters degree in Human Resource Development.

What you will notice is that all these goals are written in one sentence. This helps the goal to be clear and specific. Too much waffle can make the goal lose it's meaning.

PICK UP YOUR PEN

It's your turn now to have a go at writing some SMART goals. Think about the short term (the next 12 months) and what you personally would like to achieve over that time. Transfer these thoughts into SMART goals.

My five SMART goals for the next 12 months are:

1.

2.

3.

4.

5.

Now, check these five goals against SMART. Are all your goals Specific, Measurable, Achievable, Relevant and do they have a Timescale?

48. Use the power of your mind

Your mind is a very powerful tool, and will be extremely helpful to you in goal setting. On the next page is an excerpt from *Go MAD® The Art of Making A Difference* by Andy Gilbert. This excerpt gives a straightforward explanation as to how the mind works. This will help you to understand how you can put it to use while defining and achieving goals.

"You have two minds; your conscious mind and your subconscious mind. The conscious mind is the one you use to think with. It functions include: decision making; logic; forming judgements; and deliberate thinking. However, the conscious mind cannot cope with being aware of everything going on (most people focus on only 5-9 things happening at the same time) so the majority of information is filtered into the subconscious mind.

Your subconscious mind stores all information it receives from sight, sound, touch, taste and smell. It also records everything you do, including your words, thoughts, actions and feelings. All this information is stored in your memory, even if it sometimes appears that your conscious mind cannot remember something.

The working of your conscious mind is influenced by the subconscious mind and the information stored in it. For example, if you have lots of negative thoughts about a situation, and feel unhappy about it, these will have been stored away, and are likely to influence your conscious decisions in the future.

Your subconscious mind automatically responds to the instructions given to it by your conscious mind. It cannot act on it's own initiative. It has to be given goals to achieve, or problems to solve, before it can function. Hence, no goals – no functioning. The goals increase the alertness of your mind so that you become consciously aware of information that is relevant to what you want. This information might be already stored in your memory. If it isn't, your subconscious mind will heighten the awareness of the conscious mind to find it. Hence, the purpose of the subconscious mind is to achieve the goals and problems you define."

49. Programme your mind

The act of defining your personal goals will automatically mean that they are stored in your memory. Without you being aware of it your subconscious mind will be helping you achieve these goals – that's its job. Now, you can decide if you want to make the most of this powerful resource. We will cover more on this topic in the next section, **BELIEVE IN YOURSELF** (page 105). The following chapters (50 to 54) give you some ways to make the most of the power of your subconscious mind in setting and achieving personal goals.

"You give birth to that on which you fix your mind."
Antoine De Saint – Excupéry

---

50. State your goals positively

Your subconscious mind cannot distinguish between positive and negative. Hence, if you express your goals negatively, for example, *"I don't want to be in this job in five years time"* – your mind will focus on 'this job' first. So, if the goal was stated as, *"I want to be in a Marketing role in five years time"* – your subconscious will be helping you to seek ideas and opportunities to achieve this.

This means you need to focus on what you want, rather than what you don't want. A Go MAD® colleague of ours, Umang, had an experience which really brought home this point. He was having his first ever ride on a quad bike in the area surrounding our work premises. This area is uncultivated and includes trees, hedges, an outcrop of rocks and a pond. Umang relates how, as he started his ride, all that was going through his mind was, *"I mustn't go in the pond, I mustn't go in the pond."* Guess what happened. Yes, Umang and the quad bike ended up in the pond. He got what he focused on! This tale gives a clear message – focus on what you want – in Umang's case a dry trip – not what you don't want, i.e. a dip in the pond!

51. Think to the future

A useful tool in identifying or clarifying goals is to imagine yourself forward in time. If you can picture where you might be in five years time (or any time-frame you want to use), you can start to manage your life with the purpose of getting there. Being realistic, you cannot guarantee the exact time or the how of getting there. However, being clear on what it will be like when you do arrive at your destination is going to increase your chances of getting there! Also, you will know when you have arrived.

"If you don't daydream and kind of plan things out in your imagination, you never get there. So you have to start someplace."
Robert Duvall

You can put yourself in the future by taking the following steps and asking yourself a series of questions:

- Start off by imagining your life in five years time. Your life, as you would like it to be.
- Look at your life through your own eyes – as if you had travelled through time.
- Where are you?
- What are you doing?
- Who is around you?
- What can you see around you?
- What can you reach out and touch?
- What are you feeling?
- What can you smell?
- What are you saying?
- How are you feeling?

Visualising yourself in the future will make this activity more powerful. To undertake this you will need to make sure you are relaxed – sit comfortably and breathe slowly and deeply for five minutes. Then ask yourself each question, closing your eyes to allow for full concentration. You may want to involve someone else by getting them to read the questions to you. This will allow you to visualise the future in full detail.

Whatever method you choose, be sure to make a note of any thoughts, feelings or ideas that come to you. You can choose your own time-frame into the future if five years doesn't feel right for you.

What are you putting off? Why postpone happiness?

---

52. Remind yourself

In chapter 47 (page 91) we recommended that you write your goals. Once you do this, you will be able to focus your mind on your goals on a daily basis. You can do this by keeping them somewhere you can see them. The authors of this book keep them in a variety of places including daily planners, on bathroom mirrors and by the bedroom light switch. Choose a place that is right for you. By seeing your goals on a regular basis you will be reinforcing them in your conscious and subconscious mind.

53. Give yourself positive messages

Hands up all those people who talk to themselves (in their head or out loud). Most people will admit to talking to themselves internally. The important question is what are you saying? As your subconscious mind is taking in everything – are you encouraging or discouraging yourself?

If you say to yourself, *"I'm so useless at goal setting."* Then the chances are that you will be useless at goal setting, because that is what you are asking your mind to focus on. You can change what you say to yourself at any time. So why not tell yourself, *"I am getting better and better at goal setting."*

**The most important person you
will talk to is yourself.**

Once you are working towards your goals, use your inner voice to recognise your achievements and successes. Tell yourself you are, *"doing well."* Tell yourself you are *"getting closer to your goals."* Constantly and positively reinforce your goals and the actions you are taking to achieve them.

54. Believe it is true

You can fool your mind to believe something is true. You do this by acting as if it were true. For example, if you have a goal of obtaining a certain job or position consider how individuals in those roles behave. What do they do? How do they present themselves? What do they say? What does it feel like to be in that role? Start acting like you are already there. Your mind will make you aware of information that is relevant to that role or position, as it believes you are already there.

**"You are not what you think you are.
But what you think you are!"
Norman Vincent Peale**

---

55. Chunk down

Some of your longer-term, or complex, goals may need breaking down into smaller chunks. Breaking them down into steps or subgoals will make them seem more achievable. It will also enable you to recognise your successes on your journey to your overall goal. It will help your journey to be even more enjoyable.

Recognising and celebrating the achievement of subgoals will also develop a habit of success – both consciously and subconsciously. If you reward yourself verbally the success will be noted by your subconscious. Your subconscious will think you are a successful person. Hence, you are more likely to act as if you are successful.

You can also give yourself an actual reward or treat – whatever you fancy!

56. Involve others

To reaffirm your goals you might wish to discuss them with others. You will need to decide who is appropriate. If your personal goals impact on those who are close to you, you will need to discuss this with them. You may even want to encourage them to define some goals for themselves. Or you may wish to discuss and agree some joint goals. Kathryn, one of the co-authors, and her partner Paul have individual career goals, however they jointly agree goals that impact on their balance of life. They discuss and define goals about their life outside of work. This isn't hard work. They have a good chat over a few drinks with a bit of paper to jot their goals down.

Many organisations' individual performance review processes allow for the opportunity to discuss career aspirations. Even if the process doesn't advocate it, a good manager will talk to their team members about their career and their career aspirations. Take this opportunity to explore what is available, to discuss what it is you want and plan how you can make it happen. Remember that aspirations are not necessarily about job promotion. Aspirations will include new skills you want to learn, areas of work you are interested in and the work life balance you want to achieve.

"A single conversation across the table with a wise man is worth a months study of books."
Chinese Proverb

Disclosing your goals to others can help you achieve success. A word of warning though, be careful with whom you share your goals. Only share them with people who will encourage, support and be a positive influence for you. Don't share them with someone who will ridicule or belittle your goals. They are your goals, not theirs.

ASK YOURSELF

- Who do I want to share my goals with in my personal life?
- Who do I want to share my goals with at work?

57. Not set in concrete

Goals are not set in concrete. They are there to be reviewed, updated and amended. Your circumstances may change and you may find you no longer have a strong enough reason why to pursue a particular goal. You might want to rewrite your goal because you realise it could be SMARTer. Timescales may become unrealistic because of unforeseen circumstances. They are your goals and you can change them as and when you feel necessary. It is important that you do not become tied to goals that are no longer worthwhile. So, don't be a slave to your goals; be in control – review, amend and update them whenever you want to.

Make it a habit to review your goals on a regular basis. This will bring them to the forefront of your conscious mind and keep you on track. So in the same way that you put dates in your diary to do other tasks, do this to remind yourself to review your goals.

58. Keep them rolling

When reviewing your goals identify the times that you need to add any goals. You may be close to reaching a major goal – this will be a good time to identify your next goal. You may also need to break some of your goals into subgoals. Or, there may be new areas of your life that need direction. Whatever your circumstances keep up the good habit of personal goal setting.

> **"It is easier to go down a hill than up,**
> **but the best view is from the top."**
> **Arnold Bennett**

59. Dare to be different

Let's go back to Helen's story, which started this section. Helen dared to be different. She set herself a challenging personal goal. She was clear on what she wanted. Having identified the goal she was then able to go after it. We said at the start of the section that only 3-5 % of the population has personal goals. If you haven't already got goals why not dare to be different?

> **"Life is either a daring adventure or nothing."**
> **Helen Keller**

PICK UP YOUR PEN

Here's your opportunity to take one more step on your path to success. Commit to paper your personal goals. They can be goals relating to your work and career. They can be goals that cover other areas of your life. Remember larger goals can be broken down into subgoals. Remember to ensure they are SMART. Use the space overleaf to write them down.

My personal goals are:

Obviously, goals in themselves will not get the end result. Some action needs to be taken. The last section of the book will help you build on these goals and put together an action plan.

**"We all have possibilities we don't know about.
We can do things we don't even dream we can do."
Dale Carnegie**

CAPTURE YOUR THOUGHTS

Now we have reached the end of this section take some time to reflect on the points raised for you. You may want to consider:

- How happy am I with the goals I have identified?
- How SMART are my personal goals?
- If I haven't written down any goals, what is the reason?
- How can I ensure I regularly review my goals?

PERSONAL THOUGHTS AND REFLECTIONS

THREE ACTIONS FOR YOU TO CONSIDER

Here are three suggested actions to help you set and achieve your goals.

1. Write your goals out again. Put them somewhere you can see them on a regular basis.

2. Imagine what your life will be like when you have achieved your goals. Have a good daydream – picture it in detail.

3. Decide on the positive messages you can say internally to keep you focused on your goals. Write them down and regularly say them to yourself.

BELIEVE IN YOURSELF

The story of Darren Brooker

Darren Brooker, Manager of Data Network Engineering at One2One, is an extremely successful man. He is also very self-aware. Self-awareness is often overlooked in career management and Darren's story highlights just how significant it can be.

Prior to joining One2One, Darren had enjoyed a successful career as both a civilian employee with the police force and a self-employed IT consultant. Throughout this time he became an expert at asking himself difficult questions about what he really wanted from his career. He overcame obstacles, sought out opportunities, networked successfully and was very proactive in his career management.

Darren described how, after deciding he no longer wanted to be self-employed, he had spotted his next challenge in the form of an advert for a key position at One2One. In the process of recounting his interview strategy for this post Darren revealed just how self-aware he really was:

"I'm an introvert! Really I am. I received some excellent feedback after an unsuccessful interview I'd attended many years before. I had learnt that I'd more or less blended into the background – I was so frustrated because I knew I could have done the job so much better than the guy who had actually been successful. I promised myself, there and then, that I was never going to let that happen to me again." Darren described how from that day forward he became very aware of his natural inclination towards shyness.

"I developed a strategy. Where necessary, I could present an image of myself that would be more successful. For example, for my interview at One2One I made sure I was well prepared. I thought about the questions I would be asked and the responses I would give. I made sure I had considered the content of a presentation that I was required to give and thought about what my audience would expect from this exercise. I wore my 'confident clothes' – a zany tie and braces. I didn't go over the top but I made sure I made a statement and came across as being confident and self-assured. Finally, I thought positively all the time – took a deep breath – and got on with it!"

Needless to say, Darren's tactics worked and he was offered the job at One2One. Approximately two weeks after joining the organisation Darren had very good reason to smile and congratulate himself on his confidence strategy. Darren, his peers, and their manager (who had originally interviewed Darren for the position) all went away for a team building exercise. At this time Darren was required to complete a personality indicator. The results from this appraisal confirmed his self-assessment. He was considered introverted by nature! At this point Darren's manager exclaimed, *"You're not an introvert. You can't be an introvert. You were so confident at your interview – you definitely left a positive impression, it helped you to get the job!"*

As argued by Darren, *"Even an introvert can be confident, assertive and successful when the need arises!"* Darren has developed the ability to utilise all of his qualities. His flexibility has allowed him to manage both himself and his team exceptionally well.

"Make it thy business to know thyself, which is the most difficult lesson in the world."
Miguel De Cervantes

---

60. Know yourself

Darren's story illustrates the importance of self-awareness. He knew he was naturally an introvert and was able to do something about this in situations were he needed to be more extrovert. He also had strong self-belief that he could be confident when needed. He had the belief that he had the capabilities to achieve his goal – the job he wanted; the capability to perform at the interview and the abilities to do the job well. This self-awareness and strong self-belief acted as a firm base from which to achieve his goals. It helped to give him the energy to succeed.

"Men imagine that thought can be kept secret, but it cannot; it rapidly crystallises into habit, and habit solidifies into circumstance."
James Allen

When delivering training programmes we often ask the question, *"What are the characteristics of a successful person?"* The three characteristics - self-awareness, strong self-belief and showing confidence come up time and time again. They are key aspects of successful career management.

61.   Develop your self-awareness

Darren became aware of how he performed at interviews through feedback. Accepting feedback from others is useful in building your own self-awareness. If you respect and trust the person giving the feedback, you are more likely to accept it. Gather feedback from a number of sources. You can also self–evaluate. Look back at ways you acted or performed and assess your skills and abilities in those situations. Ask yourself the questions, *"What did I do well?"* and, *"What could I improve?"*

PICK UP YOUR PEN

Take this opportunity to build on your self-awareness. Imagine a friend or work colleague was describing you – what would they say? Reflect on your skills, qualities and characteristics.

My description of myself ....

To take this activity further, you could actually ask someone to write their description of you. Then compare it with yours. Look at what is different and what is the same. Then check out any differences and the reasons for those differences with the contributor.

**"Never underestimate your power
to change yourself."
H. Jackson Brown Jnr**

62. Identify your beliefs

Your beliefs, and therefore your self-belief, are based on your experience. Experience built up over years from what you have seen, heard, been told, or have seen others experience. Beliefs can be about circumstances we believe to be true, for example, 'There are no opportunities available.' Other beliefs are about the way we are, for example, 'I am creative' or, 'I'm not creative.' Also, beliefs can be about what we think we are capable of doing, for example: 'I would be good at managing people' or, 'I'll never be able to do that.'

**"The thing always happen that you believe in;
and the belief is the thing that makes it happen."
Frank Lloyd-Wright**

What we believe, and in particular what we believe about ourselves, can have a big impact on our careers. If you have been through the process of identifying what is important to you, then set SMART goals – if you don't believe you are capable of achieving them, you probably won't. Our beliefs impact so much because they affect our attitude and feelings, which affects our behaviour, which in turn affects the results achieved. Beliefs become self-perpetuating. If you believe you lack confidence, then you will act unconfidently, which will confirm that you find it difficult to be confident.

PICK UP YOUR PEN

Complete the following statements. Think of as many points as you can for each statement. This activity will take a bit of thought and you may want to take some time to think about the points raised.

The things I believe to be true are ....

-

-

-

-

-

I am ...

-

-

-

-

-

I am the kind of person who ......

-

-

-

-

-

My life is ......

-

-

-

-

-

My work is .....

-

-

-

-

-

Review what you have written.

ASK YOURSELF

- What are my strongest beliefs?
- How have these beliefs developed?
- Which beliefs are useful to me?
- Which beliefs are not useful to me?

63. Make your beliefs work with you

The most important thing is to identify which beliefs are working with you and which are working against you. This is the difference between limiting and enabling beliefs. Limiting beliefs will work against you. For example, Nicky, one of the co-authors, has a friend who works part-time as a team leader in a large organisation. Nicky's friend strongly believes that because she works part-time, she will never be considered for promotion. The impact of this is that she takes no steps to put herself in the running for promotion. She doesn't take opportunities that come along - *"Because, it won't make any difference."*

"All that a man achieves and all that he fails to achieve is the direct result of his thoughts."
James Allen

Enabling beliefs work with you. Andy remembers his first job after leaving school. He worked in a bank. Andy saw a future career for himself within the bank and he asked a colleague, *"How do you get on here?"* His colleague responded by saying, *"You've got to let the people at the top know."* So Andy wrote to the Chairman of the Bank telling him what he wanted. The result – Andy was put on the fast track management programme! Now, if you think about it, most people wouldn't have done that. Their belief would have been that it wasn't the right thing to do – writing directly to the Chairman – they would have been more likely to talk to the branch manager, or immediate supervisor. Their belief in the right way of doing things might inadvertantly have limited their success. Andy didn't know any different (he had no limiting beliefs about the situation), and he had strong enabling beliefs about his abilities. As a consequence he really did let the person at the top know of his desires.

Review the activity you completed in chapter 62 (page 109). Then:

ASK YOURSELF

- Which of my beliefs are limiting beliefs?
- Which of my beliefs are enabling beliefs?

64. Have good conversations with yourself

In the previous section of the book, **DEFINE YOUR GOALS** (page 81), we wrote about the power of the mind. Specifically how all the information you receive is stored in your subconscious mind. The subconscious mind then informs the conscious mind. As a consequence, any limiting beliefs you hold will be part of your information. This information will then have an impact when the conscious mind is deciding how to act.

"Your mind will give back exactly what you put in."

To accentuate your awareness of your limiting beliefs it is useful to stop and think about how you talk to yourself. Most people will admit to having a voice in their head. We call this self-talk. Self-talk is part and parcel of the information you feed into your subconscious mind. So if your self-talk about your abilities, your work, your career is negative, then it is likely these things might not be going as well as you would like. However, if your self-talk on the same topics is positive then you will feel and act positively in these areas. Notice the differences between saying, *"I'm no good at that"* or, *"My job's boring"* and, *"I am learning*

111

how to do that" or, *"I can make my work more interesting."* Positive self-talk is not about lying to yourself; it's about how you present information to yourself.

"Your own mind is a sacred enclosure into which nothing harmful can enter except by your own permission."
Arnold Bennett

Let's relate back to Darren's story. Darren knew he was naturally introverted. Now, Darren's self-talk could have been, *"I am an introvert, I'm never going to be good at interviews."* Instead he talked to himself about how he could make sure he was successful in interview situations. Also notice Darren doesn't put himself down for being naturally introverted. He accepts himself as he is. He works on displaying extrovert behaviours when needed. Positive self-talk works!

PICK UP YOUR PEN

Look back to the earlier activity in chapter 62 (page 109). Highlight any of your beliefs that have negative aspects. Using that as a starting point, identify any negative self-talk you have about your work and career. Write this in the form of statements in the left-hand column on the opposite page.

Then, identify how you could turn these negative statements into positive statements – note these in the right hand column.

My negative self-talk	My positive self-talk

If you catch yourself slipping into negative self-talk –
correct yourself – make it positive! Remember that **you**
have full control over what **you** say to yourself.

65. Identify all the positives about your career

If you are having difficulty thinking positively about your career, have a go at this next activity.

PICK UP YOUR PEN

To focus on the positives in your career, take some time to list all the good things about your career. If you have trouble identifying good things, write down the good things you would **like to have** in your career.

The good things about my career:
-
-
-
-
-
-
-
-
-
-
-

Now expand these good points into a statement about your career. This you can use as positive self-talk or to describe your career to others. If you constantly feed your mind this positive message, this will guide and direct you in your career.

PICK UP YOUR PEN

My positive career statement is:

**"One comes to be of just such stuff as that
on which the mind is set."
Upanishads**

---

66. Turn the shoulds into coulds

Sometimes limiting beliefs are developed or reinforced because of what we call the **shoulds** i.e. the way things **should** be, the way we **should** be, or the things we **should** do. For example: 'Mothers **should** stop at home and bring up the children,' 'I **should** be patient with everyone,' 'I **should** go after that job.' This impacts on your beliefs because you have a long list of **shoulds** mulling around in your head. It then becomes unclear if this is something you want or something you feel you **should** do or be.

Now, consider what happens if you turn the **shoulds** into **coulds**. So, 'Mothers **could** stop at home to bring up the children,' 'I **could** be patient with everyone,' 'I **could** go after that job.' You immediately give yourself a choice. Having a choice gives you power. Recognising the choice puts you in control. So, watch out for all the **shoulds** in your head and identify the choices you have.

**"Repeat anything often enough and
it will start to become you."**
Tom Hopkins

---

67. Ask yourself high quality questions

In the same way that you talk to yourself you also ask yourself questions. In his story, Darren says he became an expert at asking himself questions. Questions that would help him to manage his career. Questions about what he wanted from his career, the opportunities that existed for him and what he could do to be proactive. What Darren was doing was asking himself high quality questions. You too can make the most of the power of your mind by asking yourself high quality questions.

Let's consider what happens if you ask yourself poor quality questions – the answers will be poor quality. High quality questions will give high quality answers. This ensures you have your subconscious working on high quality information as opposed to rubbish. So even when you are not consciously thinking about it, your unconscious mind will still be working on those high quality questions – and coming up with the answers!

Poor quality questions tend to focus on negative aspects or put blame onto others, for example, *"Why wasn't I given that opportunity?" "Why do they always get it wrong?"* High quality questions are positively phrased. They focus on what you can do to improve circumstances.

**"You cannot take charge of the present if you are
busy reliving the setbacks of the past."**
Newman & Berkowitz

As part of our ongoing career management research we ask individuals to identify high quality questions. We now have a large database of these questions – a selection of which are below:

- What are my personal goals?
- What am I capable of?
- What gives me the greatest satisfaction?
- What do I value most about my organisation?
- What can I do to increase my happiness?
- What questions will cause me to focus most effectively on my career?
- What will I be doing in the next two years?
- What do I really want out of a career?
- What can I do to improve my present situation?
- What opportunities might there be in the career I wish to pursue?
- What opportunities can I make in my current organisation?
- What job will I be able to do in ten years time?
- What am I able to offer an employer?
- What will employers want of me?
- What impact will new technology have on my career?
- What other changes will impact on my career?
- What does my organisation value most highly?
- Who can help and support me in achieving my personal goals?
- How can I keep up to date with relevant information?
- How is my career development being helped or hindered by my current organisation?
- How attractive are my skills and experience to other employers?
- How do my current skills relate to my ultimate goals?
- How could I be proactive in developing my current role or creating a new one?
- What actions do I need to take in the short term to ensure my lifelong employability?
- How can I show the organisation my full potential?

Imagine having your mind focused on the answers to these

questions. Think about all the good quality information you will be feeding yourself.

PICK UP YOUR PEN

From this list of high quality questions pick six that, if answered, would provide you with good information to work on while managing your career. As a reminder, make a note of them below.

My six questions:
-

-

-

-

-

-

If you ask yourself a set of high quality questions on a regular basis, you will start to come up with the answers. The answers will highlight action you could take to pursue your goals and Go to Work on Your Career

68. Have enabling beliefs

Any limiting beliefs you hold may have been with you a long time. Therefore it will take some effort to change them. Darren's story highlights how he changed his self-belief from, *"I'm an introvert"* to, *"I can be extrovert and confident when I choose."* Focusing on positive self-talk will help you counteract any limiting beliefs you hold. A further step will be to change that limiting belief to an enabling belief. There are specific actions you can take to achieve this. They are as follows:

1. Identify the limiting belief. Decide whether it gives you any benefit at the moment. If not, decide to change it.

2. Imagine what it would be like if you continued with this limiting belief – what would your career/life be like?

3. Identify an enabling belief that could replace the limiting belief. Be sure you are clear on what it is.

4. Look for evidence that this enabling belief is possible. Review past actions and successes. Identify those times when you have acted as if you held this enabling belief.

5. Look outside yourself. What role models can you identify? People for whom this belief is already true. Recognise those who might think that you already hold this belief.

6. Imagine what it would be like if you had this new belief. Visualise yourself in the future with this new belief. Imagine what it is like. Picture how differently you feel. Enjoy feeling this way.

7. Use your self-talk to state the new belief to yourself regularly. For example: *"I am successful"* or, *"I am confident."* You could even say it out loud. You could also write it out and keep it in a place where you repeatedly see it.

8. As the new belief becomes embedded, allow yourself to recognise the difference.

Now, if you are cynical, you might be saying, *"What a load of rubbish – you can't change your beliefs."* Which, in itself, is a limiting belief. If you do have some limiting beliefs you want to change, why not give it a go? You never know it might just work.

ASK YOURSELF

- What limiting beliefs would I like to change?
- What am I prepared to do to change them?

"To change your attitude is to change your life."

69.   Build your own beliefs

As well as changing limiting beliefs, it is important that you reinforce your enabling beliefs. You can do this by concentrating on your self-talk. Ensure your self-talk reinforces your enabling beliefs. Continually gather evidence to support those beliefs. This can include evidence of other people acting on this belief. Make sure you recognise when you are behaving in a way that supports the belief and give yourself a pat on the back!

If you get rid of limiting beliefs and develop enabling beliefs you will be amazed at the difference it can make. If you don't believe in yourself, no one else will. Developing your self-belief in your abilities is the biggest favour you can do yourself. It will also be a crucial factor that impacts on the achievement of your personal goals.

"Success is an inside job."
Ralph M. Ford

70.   Affirm your beliefs

Some people use affirmations to reinforce their enabling beliefs. Affirmations are positive statements you frequently say. For example: *"I am a positive and confident person,"* or, *"I have all the abilities to achieve my goals."* Now you can say affirmations to yourself or you can say them out loud. Saying them out loud will make them seem more real.

Affirmations give added energy when you are establishing a new belief. It might even be that you don't believe them when you first start saying them. However, by saying them you will start acting like the belief is true. This will then reinforce the belief and you will begin to believe that the affirmations are true. A few pointers to bear in mind when using affirmations are:

- The statements should be phrased in the present tense - as if it is already happening e.g. *"I am ..."* or, *"I love .."* or, *"I have ..."* or, *"I feel ..."*

- Say them like you mean them – put emotions into your words.

- Only have a few at a time – so you are focusing on priorities.

- Say them frequently – at first, at least five times a day.

- Write them out and put them where you can see them as a reminder.

- Start with the affirmations you feel most comfortable with – perhaps ones that you already believe to be true.

- Remember they do not have to be true when you start to use them. They act as a self-fulfiling prophecy – they become true.

- Recognise when you no longer need to use them – develop new ones.

"Thoughts are energy, and you can make or break your world by your thinking."
Susan L. Taylor

> **PICK UP YOUR PEN**

Take this opportunity to create your own affirmations. What affirmations would help you achieve your personal goals? What affirmations will help you towards career success? Practise writing a few below.

My affirmations:
-
-
-
-
-
-

Having written them – why not start using them?

71. Build your confidence

Firstly, why are we talking about confidence in relation to managing your career? Because there will be times when you need to show confidence to achieve whatever it is you want to achieve. We have found, working in the career management field, that people frequently state lack of confidence as the main reason for them not achieving in the way that they want.

Secondly, what is confidence? We have commonly found that people describe it as a 'feeling'. Confidence is the feeling and behaviour that comes from having a strong self-belief. It's about how you feel internally and how that shows externally.

Everything we have said so far about self-belief will help you to build a firm foundation of confidence. You can use positive self-talk to build confidence on a regular basis; to reinforce or create an enabling belief of confidence; or in those specific situations where you would like to appear more confident.

Kathryn remembers a workshop participant recounting how she used positive self-talk effectively. Jane was preparing for her regular performance review meeting with her line manager. She felt previous meetings had not gone that well. Her negative self-talk was about how her boss never listened, how she couldn't get her point of view across and how it didn't matter what she said anyway – it wouldn't make any difference. Jane did some work on her self-talk and identified how she could make it more positive. Jane related how she approached the meeting. She had a long walk to the meeting room. All the way there she talked to herself. She was saying to herself, *"My boss may not have listened in the past but I am going to put my points across clearly and firmly. I am going to leave this meeting feeling good about how I managed it."* And she was saying these things over and over to herself. In the meeting she felt confident in putting across her views, and believed she had handled it well. All in all, the meeting was a success!

ASK YOURSELF

- What are my current levels of confidence?
- In which situations do I feel most confident?
- Are there any career management situations in which I would like to feel more confident?

If you feel that you are confident when you want to be, you may want to skip the rest of this section. If you would like to build your confidence, whatever the situation, then read on. The next few chapters will give you more ideas on how to increase your confidence.

**"No-one can make you feel inferior
without your consent."
Eleanor Roosevelt**

72.   Prepare to be confident

Refer back to Darren's story. He ensured he was well prepared. He prepared responses for the questions he anticipated might be asked at the interview and identified the needs of the audience in preparation for his presentation. He also considered what clothes were most appropriate to wear. Undertaking that amount of preparation is bound to give extra confidence.

You can also prepare through mental rehearsal. Run through the situation in your head and imagine how it will be successful. It is important to visualise yourself as confident when doing this. See yourself being confident, hear yourself speaking confidently and feel yourself being confident. To do this you will need a clear understanding of how confidence is displayed. Observe others to really tune into what confidence looks like.

**"Your imagination is your preview of
life's coming attractions."
Albert Einstein**

As well as using your imagination it is worthwhile to rehearse speaking confidently. This can be done out loud to yourself. Practise what you want to say, how you want to say it and how you want to look when saying it. An option is to involve a friend to rehearse or role-play the forthcoming event. All the authors can remember times when they have involved others in this way – to act as interviewers for jobs, an audience at presentations and a person to be approached with an idea or proposal.

73.   Focus on the positive

A good way to build confidence is to focus on the things you do well – as opposed to focusing on the things you feel you don't do well. Giving yourself lots of positive messages will increase your confidence. This doesn't mean that you don't look to improve. It just means that you also identify your strengths.

Recognising and increasing personal strengths enables you to overcome weaknesses.

PICK UP YOUR PEN

Start right now. Identify all the things you do well. Put anything you feel like on your list. It can include skills, qualities, situations where you perform to your best and situations where you act with great confidence.

The things I do well are:

Hopefully you have come up with a long list. Use it as a reminder if self-doubt starts to creep into your thoughts.

74. Talk with confidence

Notice how you and others talk when feeling confident. Notice the tone, volume and pitch. Register the kind of words used and the energy and power behind them. Imitate this in your self-talk. Imitate this in situations where confidence is required. If you sound confident, others will believe you are confident.

> **"In words are seen the state of mind, character and disposition of the speaker."**
> **Plutarch**

ASK YOURSELF

- What tone, pitch and volume represent a confident voice?
- What kinds of words display confidence?
- In what type of career situations will confidence be required?

75. Find a role model

You can involve others in helping you to Go to Work on Your Career, with or without their knowledge. Look for someone who you would describe as extremely confident. Ensure that it is someone you respect. Study them and their approach. What do they do and say that tells you they are confident. Identify what you can learn from them. Decide how you can adapt what you have learnt and apply it to yourself. We are not saying you should be exactly like them. We are suggesting that you consider adopting their confidence traits.

> **"He who can copy can do."**
> **Leonardo Da Vinci**

You could even pick a famous person to model yourself on. Why not a fictional character? Anyone whom you feel fits the bill and whom you can observe and learn from. If you choose someone you know, you have a choice. You can choose to observe without their knowledge or you can choose to let them know what you are doing. Involving them at a personal level will give you the opportunity to ask questions and delve further into what enables them to be confident. It will be your decision based on the relationship and the circumstances.

> **ASK YOURSELF**

- Who might be my role model?
- How can I make the most of the opportunities to observe them?
- How much do I want to involve them in what I am doing?

76. Take small risks

To increase your confidence, think big but act small. If being confident feels unnatural for you, start in low risk situations. Then you can slowly build your confidence to tackle the situations where more is at stake, for example, rather than starting by going to ask your boss for a pay rise (a situation many people find difficult), start by introducing yourself to someone you want to network with.

"I believe that anyone can conquer fear by doing the things he fears."
Eleanor Roosevelt

It is important to take small risks rather than large ones. This isn't because these things are going to go wrong – you will have prepared, so they will go right. It's just that it's best to start with situations in which it is easier for you to be confident. You will then be starting to gather evidence for your self-belief that you are confident. Building a strong foundation of self-belief in your ability to be confident will ensure long-term repetition and success. As you practise your new found confidence, in situation after situation, it will grow and grow. You will then reach the stage where you actually feel confident in a range of circumstances. You will then be thinking and acting big.

Remember to recognise these as *wins*. Give yourself some praise for doing well. Celebrate how well you are doing and remind yourself of all the times you have been confident.

"As long as you are going to be thinking anyway, think big."
Donald Trump

---

77. Learn from experience

You can grow your confidence by learning from your experiences. Darren's story, at the beginning of this section, shows how he reviewed his behaviour and realised what he wanted to change. Undertake a review following interactions where confidence was required. Assess what worked and what didn't work. Don't spend ages dwelling on what didn't work. Identify what would work better and move on. Internalise what you did well for the future. Add this to your picture of you as a confident person.

"Positive thinking is reacting positively to a negative situation."
Bill Havers

---

78. Get the butterflies flying in formation

Have you ever heard someone say, *"I was so nervous I had butterflies in my stomach?"* The aim is to get the butterflies flying in formation! Get them to work for you as positive energy. It's good to have nervous energy – it helps you to perform well. So, how do you get them flying in formation? By practising all the things we have suggested in this section; by believing in your ability to be confident and by acting like you are confident.

You could have a million butterflies swirling around inside you – but no one else can see them. Act like you are confident and others will react like you are confident. Remember Darren? He even went as far as to think about dressing confidently – he wore his 'confident clothes'. Act it and you will be it.

Darren also took a 'deep breath.' What's the significance of this? Firstly, that he got on and actually went for it. Secondly, deep breathing is a way of relaxing. Think back to the book section, **ACHIEVE A BALANCE** (page 74). We looked at ways of managing pressure, one of which is to breathe calmly. Part of being confident is looking relaxed. Some of the pressure management strategies will help you to achieve this. It might be worth reviewing the strategies and confirming what will work for you.

"As long as you believe in yourself, others will."
Cynda Williams

CAPTURE YOUR THOUGHTS

Once again it is time to reflect on the points this section has raised for you. Take this opportunity to note down your personal thoughts and reflections. It may help to consider the following:

- How far have I gone in identifying my limiting and enabling beliefs?
- Which beliefs would I like to change?
- What enabling beliefs would I like to develop?
- How many of the activities did I do?
- If I didn't do some of the activities, what was the reason?
- How strong is my belief that my personal goals are achievable?
- How strongly do I believe that I have the abilities to be able to achieve my goals?

PERSONAL THOUGHTS AND REFLECTIONS

THREE ACTIONS FOR YOU TO CONSIDER

Here are three suggested actions for you to take to increase your self-belief and confidence.

1. Write a list of the things you like about yourself. Plan to do this at least every three months.

2. Pick a situation where you would like to be more confident. Use the information in this section to be well prepared. Go for it!

3. Talk to yourself nicely every day.

> **"The mind is the limit. As long as the mind can envision the fact that you can do something, you can do it, as long as you really believe one hundred percent."**
> **Arnold Shwarzenegger**

CONTRIBUTION FROM
ROYAL AND SUNALLIANCE

At Royal & SunAlliance, our approach to personal development and career management is one which supports the individual who takes responsibility for his or her own learning and personal advancement.

The principle of self-directive learning is very much part of our culture. As individuals we take personal responsibility for developing the skills and capabilities we need both now and in the future. However, self-directive doesn't mean self-supportive. Royal & SunAlliance provide opportunities and plenty of encouragement while supporting individuals as they learn and grow.

The range and variety of support we currently offer and continue to develop and provide is very broad. We have on-line solutions, traditional course programmes, international programmes, and formal studies which are linked to many renowned business schools. The options available to the individual are plentiful and discussions with managers offer help and guidance in finding the best route to success for the individuals concerned.

Our employees also have the opportunity to take ful advantage of Royal and SunAlliance's Career Management Toolbox, which guides them to make better informed career decisions, and our leaders to coach and support them. It is available from both our knowledge centres, and the intranet.

We have also introduced an online 360-degree feedback process enabling, and enhancing, the gathering of data, and use of feedback. This ensures we involve others in the development planning process, and takes full advantage of the advancements in technology, and the advent of e-learning and e-business.

Our approach to leadership development is multi-faceted. We have programmes aimed at new team leaders and a follow up linked to competencies which expose the more experienced leader to real life issues and scenarios. The programmes are all 'learner centred', and incorporate action planning to enable users to implement their learning back in the work place.

Development centres form a key part of our strategy and are the start of an on-going development process which takes into account management competencies, and provides a framework for career planning. There are a variety of these available, both nationally and internationally, for individuals to use at different stages in their career.

Many of our people also choose to move across our four UK businesses, and into the international arena. The opportunity to work in different environments provides the 'icing on the cake'. It really helps to increase the confidence and flexibility of the individuals who choose to make the most of the opportunities Royal & SunAlliance offer them.

Contributed by Jacqui Nield, H.R. Development Manager

DEVELOP YOUR ABILITIES

The story of Nigel Beard

Nigel Beard, an Engineering Group Manager at Acordis, readily admits he didn't enjoy school! He left at sixteen with the ambition of getting himself an apprenticeship. *"In those days getting a good trade was seen as all important. To me an apprenticeship was a means to an end – it would give me a trade!"* Nigel soon found the academic aspect of his apprenticeship very easy; he gained little satisfaction from this but decided he must complete the apprenticeship. *"I soon realised that a simple trade wouldn't be enough for me. I had ambition, and I wasn't finding the theoretical side of the apprenticeship particularly challenging. Strangely enough completing the course showed me I wanted more."*

Nigel described his motivations to us at this point. *"There had always been milestones I set myself in my career decisions. For example, my first goal was to get myself an apprenticeship. Then serve my apprenticeship and gain some recognised qualifications – this would give me a union card that described me as a craftsman! Finally I wanted to find myself a job in a company which recognised me as that craftsman."*

After completing his apprenticeship Nigel gained employment as an engineering technician. The apprenticeship had, however, given him a taste for bigger and better things! In spite of his poor achievement record at school, he knew academically he was capable of achieving far more. *"I realised that paper qualifications had become important to me – I wanted to make up for wasting my time at school."* Nigel proceeded to enroll on courses for a variety of different technical certificates. He gained more and more experience, and had the certification to support his advances.

It was a chance meeting in a pub with two Mechanical Engineers that proved to be the next significant milestone in Nigel's career. *"After some general chit chat they asked me why I didn't want to go on to be an engineer. I explained that I had only got technical qualifications and that I had left school with no academic qualifications as such, so I didn't think I'd be able to get into a university or polytechnic. After I told them what qualifications I had got and described my work experience, they seemed to think that I would be a perfect candidate for a degree course!"*

On the basis of this conversation Nigel sent off for prospectuses and applied to many different establishments in order to study for a degree in Mechanical Engineering. He was offered a place at Nottingham Trent University. *"After going through the interview process, I decided that I wanted to stop work and study full time. I felt I owed it to myself."* Nigel made a big decision and left full time employment.

Due to the gap in his education Nigel described how he struggled with the course content for the first twelve months. He was, however, pleasantly surprised to find he passed the first crucial year. *"I thought to myself - this is ok, I can do this!"* The second year of study went much better for him - well enough to ensure he was streamed onto the Honours degree course. *"It became really important to me then to get an Honours degree, rather than an unclassified degree. This became my next goal!"*

After he graduated with an Honours degree in Mechanical Engineering, Nigel applied for several jobs and decided to accept the offer of a Plant Engineers role at Acordis. Nigel's career within Acordis progressed in leaps and bounds as the company soon recognised his ambition and potential. Nigel told us that he felt his career progression had probably been unorthodox, but that it had given him many skills he wouldn't have had if he had not completed his apprenticeship. *"Relatively speaking, I had not long left the shop floor. This gave me great insight into the problems experienced in this area. I was able to appreciate the demands and constraints experienced by the people I managed. I was literally able to lead from the front because I'd had the experience!"*

Nigel had realised from the early stages of his career that he would be in danger of getting stuck in a career rut if he settled for less than he was capable of. He acknowledged early on in his apprenticeship that a good trade alone wouldn't be enough to satisfy his needs. He was aware that at some point a greater challenge would be needed! Armed with this personal insight Nigel has taken steps throughout his career to address his considerable ambition.

"There are billions of cells in the human brain. Any neurologist will tell you we use only the merest fraction of them – a figure of less than 10% is usually quoted. Whatever your ambitions you're unlikely ever to push up against any absolute limit of your potential."
J. H. Brennan

---

79. Personal development and career management

People sometimes wonder about the difference between personal development and career management. To be honest it can be difficult to separate the two. It will really depend on what you want from your career. For some, a career is about seeking new experiences and gaining new skills. Therefore personal development is their chosen career path. Their career goals will be personal development goals.

For others, personal development is the learning and experience they require to enable them to meet their career goals. Individuals in this category tend to have specific career goals. These will be supported by subgoals, which incorporate the development activities required to keep them on track with their goals.

"Anyone who stops learning is old, whether 20 or 80. Anyone who keeps learning is young. The greatest thing in life is to keep your mind young."
Henry Ford

Some individuals will undertake development activities for the fun of it; because they enjoy learning; because it keeps their brain functioning; because there is always something new to learn.

ASK YOURSELF

- Which of my current goals are personal development goals?

80. Continue to develop

Nigel's story demonstrates the importance of continual development. To achieve his goals he needed to gain recognised qualifications. Hence achieving the qualifications became part of his subgoals. He wasn't prepared to stand still. He wanted to build on his ability with ongoing development.

Even if you stay in the same job for 40 years you will need to acquire new knowledge, skills or behaviours (we will group these together and call them abilities). Over that period of time the changes in the world and workplace will impact on the abilities you need, whatever your role. Think about all the changes that have happened over the past 40 years – in transport, communication, medicine, and technology – the list is endless. So in essence, career management requires ongoing personal development.

"The more I learn, the more I realise I don't know."
Albert Einstein

ASK YOURSELF

- What changes in the world have impacted on my career so far?
- How have I adapted to deal with these changes?
- How committed am I to continual personal development?

81. Assess your current abilities

A useful starting point is to have a good understanding of all your current knowledge, skills and qualities. Doing a stock take of your abilities will give you the foundation to Go to Work on Your Career. We utilise a variety of activities to help individuals assess their abilities and have included two of these to help you do your personal stock take.

PICK UP YOUR PEN

Activity one

List all the jobs/projects you have undertaken in the last six years.

Make a list of the personal abilities you demonstrated in these jobs or projects.

This will include knowledge, skills and personal qualities. Make sure you include everything possible. If you find this difficult, ask yourself, *"What did I do to do that job well?"* Then look at the abilities anyone would need to have to take that action. Assess and list which of these abilities you possess.

Jobs/projects undertaken:

Personal abilities demonstrated:

ASK YOURSELF

- Are my abilities specific to my organisation?
- How much value would my abilities have outside my organisation?
- How easily would my abilities transfer to other roles?

**"The journey between what you once were
and who you are now becoming
is where the dance of life really takes place."
Barbara De Angelis**

Activity two

Consider the following areas of your life and make a note of the knowledge gained.

Education:

Courses/other training experiences:

Work:

Reading/open learning/self-study/hobbies or interests:

Use the following list (it continues on the next page) to identify your top 30 skills. Give your own definition to any you don't understand. The list is not exhaustive. Feel free to add any skills. Put a circle around your top 30.

Dealing with people skills

accepting	experimenting	observing	telephoning
achieving	explaining	organising	training
addressing	expressing	overseeing	understanding
advising	guiding	persuading	updating
amusing	handling	planning	writing
analysing	identifying problems	preparing	
arbitrating	identifying solutions	presenting	
arranging	imagining	publicising	
assessing	implementing	purchasing	
auditing	improving	questioning	
budgeting	improvising	reasoning	
caring	influencing	recommending	
checking	informing	recruiting	
classifying	initiative	reporting	
coaching	inspiring	representing	
communicating	instructing	researching	
consulting	integrating	resolving	
controlling	interpreting	responding	
conversing	interviewing	risking	
co-ordinating	investigating	scheduling	
counselling	judging	selecting	
creating	leading	self-awareness	
debating	learning	summarising	
deciding	lecturing	selling to	
detailing	listening	sensing	
developing	maintaining	setting goals	
directing	mediating	speaking	
empathising	meeting	studying	
empowering	memorising	telling	
encouraging	mentoring	supervising	
enforcing	monitoring	talking	
evaluating	motivating	teaching	
examining	negotiating	team building	

Dealing with things

achieving	displaying	investigating	recommending
adapting	distributing	judging	referring
administering	editing	making	remembering
auditing	evaluating	monitoring	repairing
checking	experimenting	observing	reporting
classifying	filing	operating	researching
collecting	financing	ordering	resolving
compiling	finishing	obtaining	responding
constructing	fixing	planning	reviewing
deciding	forecasting	precision	selecting
delivering	generalising	predicting	selling
designing	generating	preparing	studying
detecting	handling	prescribing	supervising
determining	having responsibility	processing	transcribing
developing	implementing	programming	typing
devising	improving	proof reading	writing
directing	innovating	reading	
discovering	inventing	realising	

Dealing with concepts and information

accounting	diagnosing	innovating	questioning
adapting	discovering	integrating	reading
analysing	displaying	interpreting	recommending
anticipating	disproving	inventing	recording
ascertaining	dissecting	investigating	researching
assessing	delivering	learning	reviewing
budgeting	editing	maintaining	searching
calculating	expanding	managing time	sequencing
compiling	experimenting	memorising	sharing
composing	forecasting	modelling	solving
computing	formulating	observing	studying
conceptualising	generating	obtaining	thinking logically
copying	getting	organising	translating
creating	giving	originating	typing
deciding	guiding	perceiving	updating
defining	hypothesising	planning	understanding
designing	implementing	predicting	verbalising
detecting	improving	preparing	visualising
developing	increasing	prioritising	writing
devising	influencing	processing	

Having identified your top 30 skills – reduce this to your top 15. List these below as a reminder.

1.

2.

3.

4.

5.

6.

7.

8.

9.

10.

11.

12.

13.

14.

15.

You have looked at your knowledge and skills. Now take some time to identify your personal qualities. Focus on how you behave in the workplace and take into account how you interact with others. List your personal qualities overleaf.

My personal qualities are:
-
-
-
-
-
-
-
-
-
-
-
-
-
-

You should now have a list of your current abilities. This information can now be used in a variety of ways to Go to Work on Your Own Career.

**"Give a man a fish and you feed him for a day.
Teach a man to fish and you feed him for a lifetime."
Chinese Proverb**

---

82. Review your personal goals

Let's look at how the assessment of your current abilities relates to the achievement of your goals. Your abilities will have a direct impact on whether you achieve your goals or not. It is vital that you believe you either have the abilities or can develop the abilities to achieve your goals. Without this belief you are unlikely to succeed.

Question: What are you doing to develop your abilities today?

You can increase your belief in your abilities by determining the development action required in order to achieve your goals. You will then be able to write a set of development goals to support your personal goals. (If you haven't done this already.)

**"You were born with wings.
Why prefer to crawl through life?"
Rumi**

PICK UP YOUR PEN

Take this opportunity to check that you have personal development goals in place. Review the personal goals you were invited to write in the section, **DEFINE YOUR GOALS** (page 93). Jot down your thoughts to the following questions:

How will my current abilities help me achieve my personal goals?

What abilities will I need to develop to achieve my goals?

What development goals or subgoals do I need to add to my personal goals? (Remember SMART when writing goals.)

Do I believe I have the abilities or can develop the abilities to achieve my goals?

If my answer to the last question is no, what needs to happen to increase my self-belief?

83. Seek support from your organisation

Many organisations encourage line managers to have personal development discussions with their team members. If this applies in your organisation use it as an opportunity to gain support for your personal development goals. Consider how developing your abilities will be of value to the business. This could be in current or future roles. Use any personal development planning process to agree work related development goals. Discuss these with your line manager. Gain their support in seeking the experiences that will enable you to develop. Explain how your personal development will increase your value to the organisation.

Obviously, how open you are with your line manager will depend on the nature of the relationship. However, due to organisations now having flatter structures, managers and team members are being encouraged to be more open about how they wish to develop – be this inside or outside the organisation.

ASK YOURSELF

- What opportunities do I have to involve my line manager in my personal development?
- How could my manager help and support me in the achievement of my personal development goals?
- How will the achievement of my personal development goals add value to my organisation?
- Who else in the organisation can help me to achieve my personal development goals?

"Don't bother being better than your contemporaries or your predecessors. Be better than yourself."
William Faulkner

---

84. Involve others by observing excellence

Individuals we interviewed talked about how they looked to others in helping them to assess their development needs. The following steps outline how they did this.

1. Decide on your next career step. This could be upwards, downwards, sideways or out of your organisation.
2. Look around at people currently in that role. Identify those considered to be high performers by you and others.
3. Observe these people. Talk to them.
4. Gather information on:
    - their knowledge and skills
    - how they developed their knowledge and skills
    - what they believe to be the important qualities for that role
    - how they would describe the ideal person for that role
5. Make a list of all the abilities required for that role. Prioritise the list in order of importance. What are the most important abilities that would allow you to

function effectively in that role? Which are of lesser importance? Check the reasons for your order of priority.

6. Compare the list with your list of personal abilities. Ask yourself, *'How well do they match?' 'What are the gaps?' 'Which of my other strengths might compensate for any gaps?'*

7. Amend your personal goals to include any additional development needs identified.

8. Identify all the possible actions you can take to achieve your personal development goals.

9. Prepare an action plan to meet the personal development goals you identified.

"He that is taught only by himself has a fool for a master."
Ben Jonson

The research interviewees used versions of these actions both for their next career step and longer-term aspirations. If your personal goals include specific career roles in the future, you can start developing towards them now. Start identifying the abilities, add these as subgoals to your personal goals, and plan the action to take. Go for it!

85. Evaluate what organisations want

We've talked about the abilities needed to achieve your goals. We've suggested that you investigate the skills required in future roles. A further consideration is what do organisations actually want? In addition to job knowledge, what do employers want in the way of skills, behaviours and personal qualities?

Recent research with employers produced this list of the 20 most desired skills (in order of preference).

1. Ability to get things done
2. Common sense

3. Honesty/Integrity
4. Dependability
5. Initiative
6. Well-formed work habits
7. Reliability
8. Interpersonal skills
9. Enthusiasm
10. Judgement
11. Self-motivation
12. Adaptability
13. Intelligence
14. Decision-making skills
15. Oral communication skills
16. High levels of energy
17. Problem solving skills
18. Mental alertness
19. Positive attitude to work ethic
20. Emotional control

**Skills may get you to the top,
but personal qualities keep you there.**

Looking at the list you will notice that they can't all be described as skills. Items such as common sense would be better described as a personal quality. So, when looking at your personal development it makes sense to consider development needs beyond skills and knowledge. Look at all round abilities, including personal qualities and behaviours.

There are many ways to discover what abilities organisations are looking for. Discuss this with a variety of managers in your organisation. What abilities do they seek in employees? Many organisations have competency frameworks or behavioural indicators. Assess how familiar you are with the information available in your organisation. A good check is whether what is written down tallies with what people say is important. Or more interestingly, whether it tallies with the types of abilities that are rewarded within the organisation. How do people behave and what behaviours do managers encourage? Do the written requirements match with what happens in real life?

ASK YOURSELF

- What written information regarding abilities is available within my organisation?
- How does this match what is encouraged, expected or expressed by senior managers within the organisation?

"Life is but an endless series of experiments."
Mahatma Gandhi

To manage your career successfully it is also worth looking outside your own organisation. Talk to friends and acquaintances about the range of abilities and behaviours wanted in their organisations. Job adverts can keep you up to date with the skills and abilities currently required in your occupation or industry. Consider how the abilities being asked for match the expectations of your organisation.

86. Develop transferable skills

To maintain employability it is essential that you develop a range of transferable skills. Skills that can be adapted for roles in a variety of situations. Developing transferable skills puts you in an ideal position for opportunities that are yet unknown. Having a firm skill base will enable you to be more flexible in your choice of career roles. Also, if you are unsure of what you want to do, having well developed transferable skills allows a number of options to be kept open. Research has shown that the most useful transferable skills are:

1. Budget management
2. Managing people

3. Public Relations
4. Managing deadline pressures
5. Negotiating
6. Public Speaking
7. Report Writing
8. Organisation/Task management
9. Interviewing
10. Teaching/training

ASK YOURSELF

- Which of these skills do I already possess?

We have found that sometimes, particularly if someone has been in the same job for a long time, people find it difficult to realise that they have developed skills that can be transferred elsewhere. In other words, they don't realise that they have the skills to do other jobs.

An example of this is David, who attended a Go to Work on Your Career programme last year. David had been in his role as a finance team leader for 10 years. His job was being made redundant and he was looking for another position. Finance team leader roles were few and far between. He was struggling to see what else he could do. By focusing on his transferable skills, David was able to identify a number of roles well within his capability. Placing emphasis on abilities required, rather than job titles, opens up far more possibilities.

PICK UP YOUR PEN

Go back to your list of abilities identified earlier in this section (starting on page 137). Make a note overleaf of those you consider to be transferable to other roles.

My transferable skills are:

What types of jobs could I do with these abilities?

What other transferable skills will it be useful for me to develop?

If you have identified other skills to develop, add these to your personal development goals. These can be added to the goals already identified in the activity on page 143.

87. Be prepared for the future

We have already touched on the future by considering the development you need to achieve your goals. You will also need to reflect on how the world of work is likely to change. This could be organisational change or global change that impacts on your career. Future changes in the workplace for which trends have been spotted include:

- the need for continuous learning
- more emphasis being placed on team working
- more flexibility required for movement within organisations
- the need for multi-skilling
- frequent changes of job descriptions and job duties

Some of these you will have spotted in your organisation already. Thinking of more global changes consider the following:

- The first practical industrial robot was introduced during the 1960's.
- By 1982 there were approximately 32,000 robots being used in the U.S.A. Today there are over 20,000,000.
- There has been more information produced in the last 30 years than during the previous 5000.
- The information supply available to us doubles every five years.

Imagine the impact automation and information supply has had on the job market. If you study job adverts you will see new job titles every day; job titles that do not appear in a career guidance catalogue – these roles are being created daily. Therefore, some of the changes, and the likely rate of change, are difficult to predict. For example, who would have thought 20 years ago that most people would own a mobile phone? Or that so many homes would be equipped with a personal computer? It is in your best interest (employers like it too), to develop abilities that help you adapt to change. Most managers increasingly cite being flexible or adaptable as an essential skill.

A small tip – if you naturally find it hard to adapt to change, start being the one making the changes. This is better than having them foisted upon you. Get yourself used to change. Start with small changes in your everyday life. For example, walk different ways to work, break for lunch at a different time or buy a different newspaper. Look for all the changes you can make. This will start getting you used to the idea of change. This also puts you in control. You are able to adapt to change.

ASK YOURSELF THIS

- What changes have I adapted to in my working life?
- What did I do to adapt?
- How strong are my adaptability/flexibility skills?
- What do I need to do to develop these skills further?

"The days of mammoth corporations are coming to an end. People are going to have to create their own lives, their own careers and their own successes. Some people may go kicking and screaming into the new world but there is only one message there. You are in business for yourself."
Richard Schaen

---

88. Consider opportunities and threats

Let's place the focus firmly with your organisation, for a minute. If you accept that things are likely to change, this presents you with some choices. You can choose to resist the change. You can decide to go along with it (minimum enthusiasm involved). You can choose to be the one making some of the changes. You can chose to embrace change and look for the opportunities it presents you. It's your choice.

"In times of change the learners will inherit the earth, while the learned find themselves beautifully equipped to deal with a world that no longer exists."
Eric Hoffer

Deciding to make changes, or embrace changes, will usually present you with some opportunities. The downside is that change can bring restructuring and downsizing. However, change can also bring new roles, new projects and new experiences. Let's take some time to focus on being prepared for these opportunities.

PICK UP YOUR PEN

This activity helps you to match your abilities to opportunities that might arise in the future. You might already be familiar with the SWOT (Strengths, Weaknesses, Opportunities and Threats) technique. This is a variation of it – focusing specifically on your career by answering six key questions.

1. Taking into account the likely future changes in your organisation – what opportunities could arise for you?	2. What might threaten or prevent your involvement in these opportunities?	3. What abilities do you have to be able to take advantage of these opportunities?
4. How can you minimise these threats?	5. What abilities do you need to develop to be able to overcome these threats?	6. How can you maximise these opportunities and the related abilities?

> **"Great emergencies and great crises show us how
> much greater our resources are than
> we had supposed."**
> **Source Unknown**

89. Identify ways to develop

In this section of the book we have spent quite a bit of time identifying your development needs. These development needs will help you to achieve personal goals in your current role, in future roles, in preparation for change and in making the most of future opportunities. To turn this into action the next step is to identify the activities you will undertake to enable you to meet your development needs.

> **"Education is not filling a bucket, but lighting a fire."**
> **William Butler Yeats**

Looking back to the beginning of the section and Nigel's story, it is clear that he chose a very academic development route. He needed specific qualifications for the roles he wanted to undertake. It is worth noting that there are many other ways to achieve development goals. Academic qualifications will not necessarily supply you with the abilities needed in your career. From our research we have compiled a list of possible developmental activities. The majority of these can be undertaken with minimal financial cost. Here are some examples:

- Reading a relevant book for 15 minutes each day
- Shadowing work colleagues
- Researching on the Internet
- Training courses
- Observing others
- Volunteering for projects

- Being coached
- Coaching others
- Finding a mentor
- Doing voluntary work
- Watching training videos
- Completing distance learning programmes
- Listening to self-development audio tapes in the car
- Reading relevant professional journals
- Attending meetings of professional bodies
- Training others
- Asking for feedback
- Experimenting in low risk situations
- Reviewing lessons learned from mistakes made
- Establishing a network of useful contacts
- Voluntary work

"For the things we have to learn before we can do them, we learn by doing them."
Aristotle

Many people said that gaining experience was their most common method of personal development, together with looking for opportunities to do something new or in a different way.

ASK YOURSELF

- What additional developmental activities could I add to the list?
- Which of these activities have I undertaken in the past?
- How effective was that activity for me?

"Practise is the best of all instruction."
Aristotle

---

91. Choose the most appropriate development activity

You need to choose which development activities will be most effective for you. Take the following factors into account when coming to a decision over the most appropriate activities for you:

- What range of activities is available to you? Identify all possibilities.
- From the possibilities, which will enable you to meet your development need most effectively? Consider time, cost and how fully it will meet your needs.
- Which activities would best suit your desired balance of life? For example, how will it impact on your home life?
- Which activities most closely match the way you like to learn?

PICK UP YOUR PEN

Review any development needs identified by working through this section of the book. Make a note of your preferred activities to meet each development need.

My preferred developmental activities are:

91. Keep a record of your abilities and achievements

How up-to-date is your C.V.? Individuals who are serious about going to work on their careers will update their C.V.

at least every three months. Your C.V. needs to be a current summary of your key skills and achievements. It is often your first contact with prospective managers or employers. It says what you are capable of and how you add value. It is a sales document.

PICK UP YOUR PEN

Take this opportunity to develop up-to-date statements, which can be transferred to your C.V. Look back at your abilities list (page 137 onwards) and follow through the steps to develop statements of achievement.

List your top 10 skills or abilities.	Describe how you have used each skill or ability i.e. what you did.	Describe the end result of what you did – what you achieved.	Write your statements of achievement. One for each skill or ability. Describe what you did and what the successful outcome was.
1.			
2.			
3.			
4.			
5.			
6.			
7.			
8.			
9.			
10.			

These statements can form the core of your C.V. Keep adding to your list of core statements on a regular basis. Review new skills and experience; decide how you could present these on your C.V.

There are other factors to consider in producing a professional C.V. To help you with this there is an abundance of resources – specialist companies, computer programmes, websites and books.

"Don't spend so long thinking about where you are going that you forget where you are."

CAPTURE YOUR THOUGHTS

Now you have reached the end of this section, take the opportunity to reflect on the points raised. You may wish to reflect on:

- What personal development am I currently undertaking?
- What else do I want to do?
- Have I captured all my personal development goals?

PERSONAL THOUGHTS AND REFLECTIONS

THREE ACTIONS FOR YOU TO CONSIDER

Here are three suggested actions to focus you on your personal development.

1. Update, or produce, your C.V. to include all your recent achievements and newly developed abilities.

2. Each week review what you have learnt (however insignificant). Consciously identify and record your learning experiences.

3. Research the changes likely to impact on your organisation and your career. Read relevant information, keep abreast of the job market and talk to others.

"I am still learning."
Michelangelo

**"To seek personal fulfilment only outside
of work and to ignore the significant portion
of our lives we spend working would be to
limit our opportunities to be happy and
complete human beings."**
Peter Senge

CONTRIBUTION FROM ELECTROCOMPONENTS

Electrocomponents was founded in 1937 based on the principle that we would provide a service to our customers that would be second to none.

The approach has been so successful that Electrocomponents is now the first truly global high service distributor with customer operations in every major economy. Our RS brand is known worldwide, respected by customers and suppliers alike.

For more than 60 years Electrocomponents has been dedicated to a single purpose – Service Excellence. It has been successful due to the development of a clear and concise business strategy in the market.

We rely on the excellence and enthusiasm of our people to maintain our unique success. Alongside our clear business strategy, we need high calibre people who can help to deliver it! As well as recruiting aggressively worldwide to develop leadership and commercial skills, we also provide an environment within the company for self-development.

To maximise and direct the contributions of employees through the continual development of skills, capabilities and performance in order to meet the business objectives, Electrocomponents has developed a Performance Appraisal process. It is intended to gain employee commitment as to what is expected of them and ensure constructive feedback, coaching and counselling on individual performance improvement, and personal development.

To help encourage employee learning, continuous development and education and in order to meet the immediate and long-term business challenges, there are a number of initiatives such as access to an extensive Open Learning Centre and Continued Learning and Education using both internal and external centres of excellence.

The Groups commitment is to retain, develop and train it's people in order to increase skills and knowledge. Employees should also help themselves to develop by seeking new learning experiences and thinking of creative and practical ideas to improve the way in which they work.

The company believes that continued learning and education is an important part of its commitment to developing employees and argue that it:

- Contributes to enhanced performance and contribution within the business and to the employee's personal development.
- Encourages the idea of learning within the organisation as well as acquiring appropriate qualifications.
- Encourages employees to apply learning within their working environment.
- Supports the future business needs in terms of skills and employee development.

The group also encourages employees to help themselves to develop, either by seeking new learning experiences and thinking of creative and practical ideas to improve the way in which they work, or to undertake external qualifications, which will assist their career development, and help meet the future business plans and objectives of the Electrocomponents Group.

Contributed by Marie-Claude Cavelier, Human Resources Operations Manager

BUILD A SUPPORT NETWORK

The story of Ken Bew

Congratulations are in order; Ken Bew has recently received his M.B.A. – the culmination of many years of dedication and hard work. Ken is a confident and self-assured man, a far cry from the boy who left school at sixteen desperate for a job!

Ken's route to success wasn't conventional. More luck than judgement secured him a place on an electrical apprenticeship for approximately three years. He was sixteen, earning money, and learning a good trade. Ken mooched along happily until the day he received his notice of redundancy just as his apprenticeship drew to a close.

Rather than be disheartened by this turn of events, Ken chose to perceive his redundancy as a blessing in disguise. He was forced into action. For the first time he acknowledged that he didn't want to work in a factory environment. He had no choice but to seriously consider his options. After a brief spell spraying lorries, he applied for, and was offered, a job as a junior quality assurance engineer at RS Components. He readily admits he only applied for the job because it was something he could do. He had no ambitions to go into quality assurance, simply a desire to do something different. Despite its inauspicious beginnings Ken's career began to form. As his understanding about quality assurance grew, so did his interest and thirst for knowledge.

It was at this time that Ken took his first steps on his chosen career path. He learnt quickly that if you don't ask, you don't get. With this in mind he approached his manager and asked for the company's support in the event that he could find a suitable course to attend at the local college.

Ken, never doing anything by half measures, embarked on a three-year study plan. Initially he completed a one-year City & Guilds in Quality Assurance, followed by two years of twice weekly evening classes studying for the Institute of Quality Assurance exams. Ken acknowledged the huge commitment he was making to his career and planned his time accordingly. He attended night school for two evenings a week, continued to be employed full time, fitted his homework in on free evenings and weekends and helped look after his home and family.

Following the successful completion of the Quality Assurance exams, Ken took stock of his situation and considered what he should do next. He accepted a place on a one-year programme studying for a diploma in Quality Assurance. The commitment on his time was much less. More importantly, he was aware that the diploma would take him one step ahead of the competition.

This period of study coincided with a large reorganisation within the quality department at RS Components. The department was given a new focus within the business. Ken and his colleagues were given more autonomy, which presented both challenges and a welcome change. Ken recognised an opportunity for him to become a team leader within the redefined department and approached his manager. He expressed his desire to move forwards in his career and asked for support in completing a further Diploma in Management Studies. Ken felt this would help him to manage and supervise the team more effectively.

Although Ken's manager was supportive of his desired career move, he had doubts about the suitability of the course Ken had chosen. At the suggestion of the Human Resources department, Ken's manager asked him to take a 16 Personality Factor test to assess his suitability as a manager. Ken felt a little perplexed by this suggestion. However, he consented to the test to ensure his manager's support. Much to Ken's surprise his manager had a few issues with the results of the test. He felt that they highlighted some weaknesses. Following frequent discussions Ken asked his manager to give him the opportunity to demonstrate that they were not weaknesses the test had highlighted, but strengths.

Ultimately, Ken was given the chance to prove himself, and enrolled on the Diploma in Management Studies. Unlike his previous study, Ken found the course content challenging, but thoroughly enjoyable. *"The company, who supported me financially, my colleagues, and my wife, were very supportive. The diploma was a whole new ball game for me; the homework was phenomenal. I was at college for one afternoon and evening a week from 2 till 9 in the evening; I studied all weekend and the occasional evening as well. What really helped was the support network I had formed with the other students."* Ken utilised every available resource en route to completing his Diploma in Management Studies. He read books and research papers, watched videos. He used the Internet as a research tool and to communicate with his support network throughout the week.

Ken passed his diploma, *"Although the course content was hard, I thoroughly enjoyed myself and proved that I could achieve. When I finished the diploma I knew that I was eligible to do one more year to gain a M.B.A. When I started the diploma I didn't think that there was any chance of me doing the M.B.A. but as I got further into the diploma and learnt more, I began to believe I could do it, so I did."*

Unfortunately the company were unable to help Ken financially, as he wasn't yet at a managerial level. However, with the help of his manager, who allowed him to have an afternoon off work each week to attend classes, Ken decided to fund the final year himself.

"This was too good an opportunity to miss and I knew it would be a good financial investment in myself. I wanted the MBA, I never dreamt that I could achieve this but the opportunity was there and I thought I can do this."

Ken graduated in December 2000, *"I'm happy now with my academic qualifications. Each time I've come to a crossroads, I've reassessed my goals and myself. I would now like to consolidate my knowledge in the workplace for two years and then I'll reassess where I want to be. I want the jobs I have to be stepping stones to a management role at corporate level."*

"Some people come into our lives and quickly go. Some stay for a while and leave footprints on our hearts. And we are never, ever the same."
Source Unknown

---

92. Recognise the need for support

Ken's story contains many excellent points about managing a career successfully. It tells about setting goals, creating opportunities and building confidence, to name but a few. These points are covered in other sections of the book. In this section we will be focusing on building the support you will need to Go to Work on Your Career.

"No person is an island, entire of itself; every person is a piece of the continent, a part of the main."
John Donne

A large proportion of career management involves taking personal responsibility for your career. However, you don't operate in isolation. To manage your career you need the support and involvement of others. Ken sought support in many areas. He required the financial support of his organisation for his studies and needed the support of his manager to pursue his academic dreams. His manager also acted as a sounding board and challenged Ken to justify his requests. His family supported and encouraged him, allowing him guilt free time, to study. He had the support of colleagues and the other students. Ken successfully built himself a strong support network.

ASK YOURSELF

- What support do I currently need to successfully manage my career?
- What is the state of my support network?

93. Seek support for different needs

Ken sought support in a number of areas. The support you need will vary from situation to situation. It can be useful to have a well maintained support network in place that caters for these varying needs. Then, whenever you need it, the support will be immediately available.

"We not only need to be willing to give, but also to be open to receiving from others."
Source Unknown

Now, you might say, *"I'm perfectly capable of managing things for myself. I don't need any support,"* and some people are incredibly self-sufficient. However, having the appropriate support can help you manage your career more efficiently and effectively. Besides, it's good to know that there are people you can turn to and people who are there cheering you along.

"The applause of a single human being is of great consequence."
Samuel Johnson

PICK UP YOUR PEN

There will always have been people in your life and career who have been there to provide support. This might include parents, carers, family, friends and colleagues.

Take some time to stop and take stock of who makes up your current support network. Also, consider the type of support they provide. You will possibly find that you approach different individuals for different types of support. Identify who you seek support from by considering the support areas highlighted.

SUPPORT SOUGHT/OFFERED	NAME
1. Someone who listens.	
2. Someone who will give honest and constructive feedback.	
3. Someone who helps to generate ideas.	
4. Someone who asks you high quality questions.	
5. Someone who provides positive suggestions and options.	
6. Someone who has their own effective support network.	
7. Someone who is a valuable source of information.	
8. Someone who can give financial advice.	
9. Someone who will help you to see the funny side of things.	

10. Someone who will challenge you and your ideas. 11. Someone who will provide practical help. 12. Someone who values you. 13. Someone who you can discuss your career goals with. 14. Someone who will encourage you to take action. 15. Someone who will coach or mentor you. 16. Someone who is a good friend. 17. Someone who cheers for you. 18. Someone who cares for your well being.	

ASK YOURSELF

- Are there any surprises?
- Who else is in my support network and what support do they provide?
- Does anyone provide support in more than a couple of areas? What are the implications of this?
- What gaps are there in my support network?
- Who potentially could fill those gaps?
- How would I like to change this support network?
- How can I make more effective use of my support network?

"A dwarf on a giant's back sees further than both."
Source Unknown

94. Ask for help

You probably already have relationships with the majority of people you want in your support network. If you wish to change, or add to, your support network you may need to build additional relationships. Some of these relationships may be more formal. For example, your manager will have some responsibility to support you. You can then decide if you wish to extend this relationship to areas that aren't identified as managerial responsibilities.

**" We make a living by what we get,
we make a life by what we give."
Winston Churchill**

You can build your support network by seeking help. Most people like to be asked for help or advice and enjoy giving in this way – it gives them value. Be careful that you don't place others under pressure by constantly seeking their help or support. Know when enough is enough, and recognise when it's time to ease off or to seek support elsewhere. This support is often given free of charge, so respect the needs of others.

95. Be your own coach

Remember to support yourself. Review the list in chapter 93 (page 167), rephrasing the items as questions to support yourself. This might sound a bit strange so we will give you some examples:

- How do I give myself honest feedback?
- How good am I at challenging myself?
- What do I do to cheer myself on?
- How do I care for my well being?
- How much do I value myself?

"The greatest gift is a portion of thyself."
Ralph Waldo Emerson

One area of support is having someone who asks you high quality questions. If you remember back to the section **BELIEVE IN YOURSELF** (page 116), we introduced the concept of high quality self-questioning. Asking yourself high quality questions effectively means you are coaching yourself. Good coaches will coach others by asking questions and listening. Therefore, if you can ask yourself decent questions, you can coach yourself. In the same way that you might book a coaching session with someone, book a coaching session with yourself. If some of your questions are difficult to answer, leave them for your subconscious mind to mull over.

When consciously coaching yourself be sure to jot down the answers that you come up with. Keep a record of your ideas, options and ways forward. All this information will help you to create and review your career goals and actions.

96. Show appreciation

This message is short and sweet, but very important – remember to say thank you for the support you receive.

You never know what happiness a simple act of
appreciation will bring.

---

97. Give in return

Having thought about how others support you, consider how you support others. You can be instrumental in helping others with their careers. Going to work on your career isn't about being selfish. It is about considering how you interact with others. If you want support you will need to give support in return. The danger of it all being one way is that others will see you as a *taker* - remember to be a *giver* as well. At the same time, be aware of taking on too much. It is possible to get so caught up in supporting others that you forget about yourself. Go for a balance.

"Great opportunities to help others seldom come, but small ones surround us every day."
Sally Koch

PICK UP YOUR PEN

Let's look at whose support networks you play a part in. The areas in this activity are the same as the ones identified when considering your own support network. Review each area and identify who you are supporting.

SUPPORT OFFERED	NAME
1. Who do I support by listening?	
2. Who do I support by giving honest and constructive feedback?	
3. Who do I support by generating ideas?	
4. Who do I support by asking high quality questions?	
5. Who do I support by providing positive suggestions and options?	
6. Who do I share my support network with?	
7. Who do I support by being a valuable source of information?	

8. How qualified am I to give financial advice?

9. Who do I help lighten up by seeing the funny side of things?

10. Who do I support by challenging them and their ideas?

11. Who do I support with practical help?

12. Who do I support by valuing them?

13. Who do I support by discussing their career goals?

14. Who do I support by encouraging them to take action?

15. Who do I coach or mentor?

16. Who do I support by being a good friend?

17. Who do I support by cheering for them?

18. Who do I support by caring for their well being?

ASK YOURSELF

- How active am I in supporting others?
- What energy and enthusiasm have I got to support others?
- What would I like to change about the way I support others?
- What action would I need to take to make these changes?

**"No-one is useless in this world who
lightens the burdens of others."
Charles Dickens**

CAPTURE YOUR THOUGHTS

Having reached the end of this section take the opportunity to make a note of those points highlighted for you. You may wish to consider:

- How effective is my support network?
- How effective am I at supporting others?
- What do I want to be different?
- What actions can I take to make these differences?

PERSONAL THOUGHTS AND REFLECTIONS

THREE ACTIONS FOR YOU TO CONSIDER

Here are three things you can do to build a more effective support network.

1. Discuss your career aspirations with your manager. Discuss ways he or she can support you in going to work on your career.

2. Thank those people who have supported, or still support, you. A bit of appreciation goes a long way.

3. Act on the areas in which you lack support. Approach others and ask for help.

"We cannot live for ourselves. A thousand fibres connect us with our fellow men; and along these fibres as sympathetic threads our actions run as causes, and they come back to us as effects."
Herman Melville

CREATE OPPORTUNITIES

The story of Mark Christer

If we had to sum Mark Christer up in a few words, we would refer to him as, 'A creator of career opportunities.' Whilst Mark got his first taste of opportunity creating while he was a University undergraduate, a marvellous example of his proactivity occurred not long after he joined Royal and SunAlliance.

Mark was part way through a MBA when he went to work for Royal and SunAlliance. As part of his degree he completed a dissertation on the impact of e-business in the UK Insurance market. Now while most people might send a courtesy copy of the dissertation to their manager, how many would take the steps Mark did? Setting his sights high, he made sure that both the Group Chief Executive and the U.K. Managing Director of Royal and SunAlliance received a copy of his completed report. Mark also invited them to challenge and comment on his conclusions!

After receiving a copy on a Friday afternoon, the U.K. Managing Director returned his comments to Mark on the Monday morning. As predicted by Mark, e-business was an extremely relevant topic within the company and the Managing Director had spent the weekend looking over Marks dissertation. You might say, *"So what?"* – It may surprise you to know that based purely on the merit of his dissertation, Mark was offered the position of E-Business Manager!

We also discovered that Mark had unwittingly used this self-marketing strategy once before, and with great effect. As part of his undergraduate degree in Business Computing, Mark completed a year working in industry. During this time he was asked to investigate and report on a runaway management project. As part of his research he contacted a large London based consultancy that specialised in runaway project management. They were helpful and gave him lots of good advice. Mark told us how, as a matter of courtesy, he sent a copy of his report to the company that had helped him. His report obviously left an impression! As a direct consequence of receiving the report the Consultancy took the unusual step of approaching Mark, while he was in his final year at university, to offer him a job after he graduated. The job offer was unconditional – it was based purely on the merit of the report Mark had sent them. Now consider, do you know of anyone who has been head hunted from university? Mark had obviously learnt from this early experience. The same self-marketing principle had also gained him a promotion to E-Business Manager. It pays to be proactive!

> **"There is no security in life, only opportunity."**
> **Mark Twain**

98. Be proactive

Mark created his own opportunities. It would have been easy to think, 'It's not worth doing, no-one will take any notice.' However, Mark was taken notice of and look at what it got him – a job offer straight from university and a new role in his current organisation. He made sure he created his own opportunities rather than waiting for them to come along.

Now you might say, *"It's alright for him."* He was studying, writing reports and had something to give them. This is true. However, there is more than one way to create opportunities. Also, opportunities may just appear from nowhere and you have to make sure you grab them. The question is do you want to spend your time waiting for something to happen, or do you want to do something to make things happen?

ASK YOURSELF

- What am I currently doing to proactively manage my career?
- In managing my career what opportunities have I made?
- What opportunities have emerged that I have taken?

> **The opportunities are there.**
> **They just need making or taking.**

Think about someone you regard as being successful in his or her career. It may be someone well known like Richard Branson or it may be someone you know personally (if you don't know Richard Branson personally of course!) Someone you would describe as a 'career star'. They manage their careers so successfully that they shine and stand out from the rest. How much do they make happen by asking, proposing and doing? Or how much just happens out of the blue? We bet that if you really spend some time thinking about this you'll realise that they are successful because of what they have done. They didn't hang around waiting for success – they made their own success.

"A wise man will make more opportunities than he finds."
Francis Bacon

---

99. Remember you always have a choice

Managing your career is about being proactive; it's about making things happen; it's about taking personal responsibility for creating your own future. Does that sound a bit scary? Realising that you can make things happen for yourself; that if things go wrong you can't blame others. That it's down to you.

"The difficulty in life is the choice."
George Moore

If you remember nothing else from this book always remember **you have a choice**. You always have the choice to do something or to do nothing. At times it can be hard to see the choice because you might not like the options. However, it is important to recognise that when you do nothing, you are still making a choice and it's your choice.

100. Identify your choices

On numerous occasions when we have been delivering career management programmes, participants have expressed how unhappy they are in their current job but can't do anything about it because of ...., and out comes a list: the mortgage; their partner; they like the amount of money they earn; they haven't the skills to do anything else and so on and so on. They are able to come up with lots of reasons as to why they can't do anything about their situation.

Imagine, if they turned that around and came up with a list of all the choices they have: to look for ways to enjoy their job more; to propose other work they could do within the organisation; to sell their house; to take a cheaper mortgage; to look for a job they enjoy that is less money; to retrain or study to acquire additional skills. The list could be endless.

Choice not chance determines human destiny.

What they are failing to see is that they do have a choice. We help our participants to identify these choices. The outcome may be that they don't like the choices. However, they start to understand that they are in control and they are making a choice by deciding to stay where they are. At this stage they may decide to work out how they can enjoy their job, rather than move on.

101. Take control of your career

Mark's choices have been to create his own opportunities rather than wait for something to happen to him. He is taking control of his career and choosing to be proactive.

So, if you ever feel that you do not have a choice in what you are doing with your career, take some time to sit down and really consider if that is the case. Be aware that you may not want to take up some of the options available, but realise that there are possible alternatives to the situation.

ASK YOURSELF

- How happy am I with my career at this current time?
- If I am unhappy, what alternatives are there to the present situation?
- Which of these options (choices) is practical for me to pursue?

The choice is to make a choice or to carry on pretending there is no choice.

---

102. Be career responsible

An element of choice, while managing your career, relates to taking responsibility for moving your career forward. Choosing which actions to take – or not to take.

**"A man is as big as his decisions."
Winston Churchill**

Over the last five years our career management research has included discovering the actions people take to be proactive in managing their careers. We have also sought opinions when delivering presentations to professional bodies. Over 200 managers and human resources professionals have been asked the question, *"If a person takes responsibility for their career what would they be proactive in doing?"* From this question we have gathered over 100 different answers. Overleaf is a list of 25 of the most common suggestions made.

PICK UP YOUR PEN

The following activity will help you to measure your current level of career responsibility. Look at the list and highlight those actions you already take, annotating the relevant column. Then go through the list again and highlight those actions you would benefit from taking by marking the relevant column.

Career Responsible Actions	Already doing	Worth doing
Updating my C.V. at least every six months		
Identifying my own personal development needs and formulating a personal development plan		
Linking my development needs to organisational objectives		
Building and maintaining a network of useful contacts		
Researching organisational future strategy		
Searching out role models – in career management and future roles		
Keeping abreast of changes that impact on my career		
Developing personal adaptability and flexibility skills		
Determining my career goals and having a written career plan		

Planning in time to regularly review my career goals and plans		
Looking at positions advertised to benchmark my skills against current market needs		
Connecting with online career related internet sites		
Finding myself a mentor or coach		
Working on a list of career action steps each month		
Aiming to be in the top 20% of my profession (the top 20% are always employable)		
Remembering that life is not a four lettered word spelled w-o-r-k		
Requesting feedback on my skills and performance from my manager and others		
Keeping a development diary or log		
Discussing my career goals with my partner and family		
Letting my organisation know what I want to achieve with my career		
Looking for new ways to do old things		
Undertaking continuous developmental activities		
Managing upwards by understanding the needs of my boss		

Identifying my transferable skills		
Marketing my skills and experience within my existing organisation and network		

ASK YOURSELF

- How useful have the actions that I have already taken been in progressing my career?
- What else do I definitely want to do from the list that will help me to manage my career?
- Which one action from the list would give me the greatest benefit?

103. Consider the worst that could happen

Sometimes we choose not to take action, or to create opportunities, because we imagine all sorts of things. For example:

- What if it goes wrong?
- What if they think I'm pushy?
- What will others think?
- What if it's not good enough?

Have you spotted the common theme?

What is being imagined is all negative stuff.

What about imagining:

- Won't it be great when it goes right?
- They'll be pleased I've taken the initiative.
- My friends and family will be really excited for me.
- I'm really happy with what I've done.

"You won't get a six if you don't throw the dice."

Here's a challenge for you to consider. Really and truly, **what's the worst that could happen?**

Let's take Mark's scenario. What's the worst that could have happened? The worst would probably have been the people not reading the reports he sent to them or not liking his ideas. Consider what this would have meant for Mark. He would have been no worse off than not taking action. And at least he would have known for himself that he had exercised his choice and made the effort to do something.

"Our doubts are traitors and make us lose good we oft might win by fearing to attempt."
William Shakespeare

Now, we're not saying go off and take silly risks. We're saying don't let all the things you imagine that could go wrong put you off creating an opportunity for yourself.

PICK UP YOUR PEN

Take some time to think about the opportunities you could create for yourself if you choose to take some action.

In the table overleaf, use the first column to list all the possible actions you could take to create opportunities for yourself. This activity might take a bit of thought and we encourage you to think as widely as possible. Examples of action you might take could come from the list of career responsible actions shown in chapter 102 (page 180). Or it might be something you've been thinking about doing for a long time. Perhaps you've been putting it off because you have been focusing on it not working out successfully.

Use the second column to write down the worst that could happen if you took this action.

Lastly, turn this around and focus on the best that could happen if you took this action.

We have given an example to help you get started with this activity.

Actions to take	What's the worst that could happen?	What's the best that could happen?
Example: Ask a senior manager at work to be my mentor.	She says, *"no"* and thinks I am a bit cheeky for asking.	She says, *"yes"* and agrees to meet me on a regular basis. By applying her advice I get the job I always wanted.

Having completed your list, run through it and consider the following questions:

> **ASK YOURSELF**

- What would it be like if all the best that could happen actually happened?
- What am I prepared to take forward from my list of actions?

"A lot of successful people are risk takers. Unless you are willing to do that, to have a go, to fail miserably, and have another go, success won't happen."
Phillip Adams

---

104. Become a surveyor and a proposer

A key career skill linked to creating opportunities is called surveying and proposing. This is a method to make improvements to the business and create a role or new experience for you. Surveying and proposing is essentially a three-stage process.

Step one: Observe

Take a look around (survey) the organisation you work for or maybe an organisation you would like to work for in the future. Look for areas that are open for improvement, improvements that would make or save the organisation money. Obviously saving or making money is close to any organisation's heart.

Step two: Think of an idea

For example:

- Are there any new processes or procedures that would improve production?
- Is there a way to increase customer satisfaction?
- What can be done to cut down the time needed to do certain work?

- Could teams be better organised or managed in a different way?

Step three: Propose

You then suggest (propose) your idea or the action to take. Part of your proposal will include your role in taking forward the idea. This means that if there is an area of work you would like to get involved in you can make this happen. You will be creating a role for yourself. You will have your own reason for wanting to move into that area of work. This could be anything from earning more money, or a great opportunity to build on your abilities.

**"A crank is a man with a new idea –
until it catches on."
Mark Twain**

Doing this may take some time and effort. It won't just be a case of just having a look and then coming up with an idea. You will need to research, investigate, benchmark, and maybe put together a business case for your idea. This means it is important that you think about your reason why. How strong is your reason for wanting to progress your career through that area of work? Have you got the motivation and enthusiasm to sell your idea and then to see it through?

If we think back to Mark's story at the being of this section, Mark had a strong interest in e-business. By forwarding his report to the Managing Director he ended up with a job he wanted to do and would enjoy. This isn't about being selfish, because it ties in with what the company needs. They have ended up with a motivated and knowledgeable E-Business Manager. Surveying and proposing links business benefit with your career aspirations.

> **"The meeting of preparation with opportunity
> generates the offspring we call luck."**
> **Anthony Robbins**

PICK UP YOUR PEN

Use the space provided to note your thoughts on the
following questions. This will start to give you some insight
as to how surveying and proposing will be an effective
career skill for you to employ.

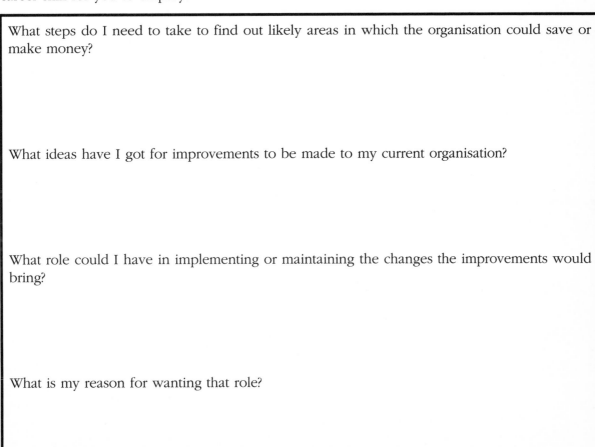

What steps do I need to take to find out likely areas in which the organisation could save or
make money?

What ideas have I got for improvements to be made to my current organisation?

What role could I have in implementing or maintaining the changes the improvements would
bring?

What is my reason for wanting that role?

How strong is my reason?

What would I need to do to be in a position to take this idea forward?

Who would I need to influence to take my ideas forward?

What would be the best way to communicate my ideas?

If you are looking to move organisations, you can apply the same questions externally to any company. You can then approach that company with your ideas and the suggested role you would play in implementing the ideas.

One of our associate consultants, who is self-employed, obtains new work with clients in the retail market by spending time in retail outlets. He looks for areas of improvements and then contacts the Chief Executive saying he knows how they can increase their profit by 10% (or whatever amount is achievable). Do you think the Chief Executives are interested in hearing the ideas of a stranger? Yes, when it comes to making money. Nine times out of ten they are prepared to listen to his ideas and take them forward.

So our colleague is not only helping these companies, but also managing his own career very successfully.

"In all human affairs there are efforts, and there are results, and the strength of the effort is the measure of the result."
James Allen

---

105. Make homework a habit

Not all opportunities can be made or foreseen. Doing a bit of homework can put you in the best position to make or take opportunities.

Opportunities are made or taken, they don't just happen.

You will have heard people talking about succeeding because they were in the right place at the right time. Invariably this is because they have done their homework, thus ensuring they are in the right place at the right time.

We recall Anna, a participant on a Go to Work on Your Career programme. She didn't have a clue what she wanted to do with the rest of her working life. What she did know were the things she enjoyed doing, and the things she wanted from a job. These included helping others, having flexibility in her working hours, using her own initiative and house hunting. These elements might seem a strange combination, however Anna planned to do some homework and work out how these components could be brought together.

So, Anna left the programme, talked to people, did some research and found a gap in the market. This gap was for someone to look for houses for business people, and their families, who were being relocated from other areas of the

189

country. Anna now runs a successful business providing a house hunting service. She saves others the time it takes to house hunt by doing it for them and presenting them with a range of options within their specifications. By starting from scratch Anna created a job that met all her personal requirements.

PICK UP YOUR PEN

Take some time to reflect on what homework you need to do. Review the following list of suggestions. Determine what relates to your current situation and identify what you need to do.

Possible areas for homework include:

- Research the job opportunities available internally and externally.
- Research the gaps in the market for the services you can provide.
- Update your job hunting and self-marketing skills.
- Become familiar with the selection process within your organisation.
- Research the people in the role you want – what are their abilities? What have they done to obtain that position?
- Identify how people have been recruited into the roles you want.
- Research the trends and changes in your field of work.
- Identify how external factors are impacting on your organisation.

Looking at the above list – What homework do you need to do?

**Put yourself in the best position for the
position you want to be in.**

106. Make the most of opportunities

When doing the research for this book, the words
'opportunity' and 'opportunities' came up time and time
again. For many individuals the success of their careers
hinged on the opportunities they had created or taken.

**"Opportunity does not have a tail –
you cannot run after it."
Indian Saying**

At the beginning of this book we talked about having a
career strategy. We stressed that part of having a strategy is
'taking advantage of opportunities as they emerge.'
This means you need to be on the look out for
opportunities. The opportunities that emerge may not
exactly match your goals. The secret is to be flexible. What
will that opportunity give you – experience, enhanced
abilities, a step in the right direction? Look for what it will
give you rather than what it won't give you. Having done
your homework – you will be in the best position possible
to make the most of opportunities.

CAPTURE YOUR THOUGHTS

Having reached the end of this section take some time to
relate your situation to the learning points that have come
out of Mark's story.

Note any points you want to remember and summarise any
action you want take. Remember you can create your own
opportunities.

PERSONAL THOUGHTS AND REFLECTIONS

THREE ACTIONS FOR YOU TO CONSIDER

Here are three suggested actions for you to think about in creating your own career opportunities.

1. Research areas for improvement within your organisation. Identify options to be researched in more depth.

2. Review the opportunities that have come your way over the last two years. Identify the action you took to make the most of these opportunities. Identify what more you could have done to make the most of these opportunities.

3. If you ever hear yourself complaining about work, recognise the choices you are making. If you don't like what is happening, identify what choices you have. Choose whether or not you want to act on these choices.

"Only those who risk going too far can possibly find out how far they can go."
T.S. Eliot

CONTRIBUTION FROM ACORDIS ACETATES

When being invited to make this contribution, I sat down and thought 'What would be most useful to input to a book on career management?'

Then I started thinking about how careers have changed. Particularly over the last 15 years, and how much the world of work has altered since I first started on my career path. I was specifically thinking about how the expectations of employers and employees have changed. We all know there is no longer a job for life, but what has this been replaced with? How has the advent of flatter organisational structures impacted on organisations and individuals' views of career management?

I want to give a snapshot view of career management from an organisational perspective. To describe how Acordis Acetates support their employees in their career development and what is expected in return.

A question that comes up on a regular basis when talking about career management is, 'Who is responsible for an individual's career?' Usually the views vary between, 'It's the organisation's responsibility to help people progress,' and, 'It's totally up to the individual.' At Acordis we like to describe the individual as being responsible for their career. After all, who's career is it? However, we would argue that as an organisation we have a responsibility to support individuals in their career development, especially if we want to develop skilled and committed people able to meet the current business challenges. So, the responsibility lies with the individual, as only they can determine what their career aspirations will be. However we will provide support in a number of ways. We have to recognise that as a company we are not always able to provide the opportunities and experience being sought. However, we can help by aiding individuals to actively manage their careers and consider the options available.

The impact of there no longer being a job for life changes the psychological contract, the unwritten and unspoken expectations between an employee and employer. The 'job for life' needs to be replaced with a psychological contract of 'we will provide the opportunities for you to develop the necessary skills and abilities to fulfil your role and enable you to remain employable'. Perhaps the organisation would like to provide a job for life for everybody and in many cases has done so, however we need to be realistic. In an ever increasingly competitive and changing world we have to ensure that we don't make promises that are impossible to fulfil.

At Acordis we provide a structure to support our people in managing their careers. The Performance Assessment and Personal Development Planning processes enable individuals to explore development and career aspirations with their line managers. We seek out opportunities for employees to experience, which could potentially be lost due to the flatter organisational structure. We have instigated career management workshops, giving participants the personal time to reflect on their careers, to consider options, to establish personal goals and widen their perspective on making a difference to their career.

So by providing this support what do we expect from employees in return? We expect people to take responsibility, to think about what they want from their careers and articulate this in discussions with their line managers. If we as employers are not aware of individual needs, there is little we can do to meet them. We will create opportunities, and we look to employees to seek out and create opportunities for themselves. We encourage individuals to recognise the impact of a less hierarchical work structure on their careers. We are looking for them to identify, with our help, other ways to seek those experiences that will enable them to personally develop.

Career management is a partnership between the employee and employer. Employees need to take control of their careers, and employers need to help employees understand how careers can be managed. Career development is not just about upward job promotion, it includes personal development, gaining experience, life balance and job satisfaction. If individuals manage their careers with the support of their organisation both sides will benefit. Employers can best help the people in their organisations by encouraging them to be proactive and take responsibility in managing their careers.

Contributed by Trevor Smith, H.R. Manager - Training & Development

MARKET YOURSELF

The story of Rebecca Denning-Southern

Rebecca leaves no stone unturned when she sets out to achieve something. Rebecca's story highlights the practical ways we can make ourselves seen – seen so well that we literally stand out from the crowd!

The first inkling we got that Rebecca was very driven on her road to success was when she told us the tale of how she went about getting a job in her chosen field – the insurance market. She was unhappily employed in a bank and had given herself two days to find a job in the insurance sector. Two days! – What, we might ask, can one person achieve in just two days? Prepare to be surprised and read on!

Rebecca, armed with the names and addresses of all the large insurance companies and reputable employment agencies, her Curriculum Vitae, and a mental script of what she was going to say to people, began a grand tour of her preferred geographical area – Bristol. In the space of two days she knocked on every door that she felt could possibly help her to find the job she sought. She asked receptionists if there were any possible openings within the company, if she could leave her C.V. for the records, if anybody was free to show her around the offices, and if anyone from Human Resources or Personnel could spare her five minutes of their time so she could tell them personally what skills she had to offer the company. Rebecca explained, *"I worked fifteen miles away from Bristol at this time. Getting two days off had been a nightmare and I only had a few days holiday anyway...I knew that I would have to condense my job hunting into two days and make it happen."* Can you imagine knocking on over twenty doors, in two days, on a quest for a job? Have you ever wanted anything this badly?

Following Rebecca's Bristol blitz she was offered several jobs – she was now in the position to make a choice! Rebecca accepted an offer of employment from Royal and SunAlliance as a junior administrator.

Within a few weeks of beginning her job, Rebecca began making conscious decisions, *"I soon worked out that if you want to get on you have to pester the right people at the right time – saying 'Hey look at me, I can offer some value'. I remember several occasions and examples, where if I had just sat there and carried on nothing would have happened – so I went out and made the opportunities for myself."*

Rebecca volunteered to do tedious jobs that needed sorting and she looked for better ways of carrying out procedures. She would drive things forward and make changes. People started to realise the benefits of the changes she had applied and the next time something needed sorting they approached her. If Rebecca saw a project developing in a different area, she approached those in control and asked to become involved…. slowly but surely Rebecca raised her profile within Royal and SunAlliance. *"Every time I could see a little opportunity – it may have been a floor away, a building away or a city away – my 'radar' would detect it and I'd volunteer."*

Throughout Rebecca's career at Royal and SunAlliance she has employed the same methods on her route to success – be seen, be heard and be proactive!

"Consider the turtle. It makes progress only when if sticks his neck out."

---

107. Stand out from the crowd

This story highlights how marketing yourself can help you get what you want from your career. Rebecca was unhappy with where she was working and knew the type of work she wanted. She was prepared to go out and sell herself and it worked!

She has recognised and applied a key career management skill – the need to get yourself noticed, for all the right reasons. In this section we will look at what you can do to ensure you stand out from the crowd.

"We must dare, and dare again and go on daring."
Georges Danton

---

108. Identify the right people

Marketing yourself isn't about being noticed by everyone all the time – you'd probably soon get on people's nerves. It's about you considering:

- Who are the people that you want to be noticed by at any given time, dependent on your career goals?
- How could they help you with your career?
- How can they get to know who you are and what you offer?

**"Success is 5% what you know
and 95% who you know."**

Let's make a comparison to product marketing and imagine yourself as a product. Marketing of products is targeted at the people who are likely to buy, at the time they are likely to buy. You'll have seen the adverts on television and recognised who they are targeted for. For example: the smaller sporty cars have adverts showing youthful women with the emphasis on them gaining their freedom. Who do you think the advertisers have identified as the most likely buyers of these cars?

Also, consider who has influence on the buyers. When are all the adverts for toys shown on television? Early morning, when children's programmes are on. On the whole it isn't the children who have the purchasing power, it's the parents or carers. So why not show the adverts when more adults are watching? Obvious, isn't it? Because it's the children who will influence (pester, whine, cry, sulk and plead!) the adults to buy.

You might be asking – "what's this got to do with me marketing myself?" This comparison raises a number of points. Firstly, determine who your target market is – who you need to notice you. Consider when is the best time to make approaches to others. This will be dependent on your needs and being respectful of their time. Lastly, consider what individuals are known by your direct contacts. This contact might be able to influence on your behalf, or introduce you to someone who can provide you with what it is you need. Later in this section we will look at the skill of networking and build on this point.

109. Make the most of indirect contacts

Let us give you an example of how an indirect contact can help you to reach the person you need to. Alan came to a one to one coaching session with Andy with the following challenge. Alan really wanted the opportunity to move departments and build his skills in the area of marketing (rather appropriate to this section of the book). However, the Marketing Manager was new to the company and Alan hadn't got to know her. In fact he hadn't even spoken to her. As well as this, the marketing team were on a different site to Alan's team – so chance encounters were few and far between.

Alan had discussed what he wanted with his own boss who was happy to support him in his move. His boss said that he would have a chat with the Marketing Manager. Alan waited and waited but nothing happened, so he asked his boss what was going on. It turned out that his boss was unable to see the Marketing Manager. She was always busy and he had been unable to get an appointment through the personal assistant.

During the coaching session Alan decided it was time to take things into his own hands. He identified who else apart from his boss would be able to get him in to see the Marketing Manager. He had found out that his boss had found it difficult to make an appointment. The Marketing Manager's personal assistant was really good at her job, particularly at protecting her manager's time.

So, Alan planned out a strategy to win over the personal assistant. He went away from the coaching session and started to build a relationship through phone calls. He explained his reasons for wanting a meeting. He called in and had a chat with the personal assistant, feeling that face to face contact would build the relationship. All in all, he sold himself to the personal assistant. It took some time, but in the end he got that appointment. He fedback to Andy that building a relationship with the personal assistant not only got him the appointment with the Marketing

Manager – he actually found out that she had spoken very positively about him to the Marketing Manager. Alan was initially given the opportunity to become involved in a one off project and then was offered a post within the Marketing team.

So, don't be put off if you can't immediately get to see the person you want to. Think about how you can build relationships with those who could make that introduction.

"Nothing happens by itself. It will come your way once you understand that you have to make it come your way, by your own exertions."
Ben Stein

---

110. Map out your relationships

We have mentioned that you don't need to get yourself noticed by everyone. At different times there will be different people who will help you with your career. For now let's focus on your current position.

PICK UP YOUR PEN

Think about where you are at the moment with your career. Who might help you either inside or outside your organisation? The term 'help' can cover anything that might help you move your career in the way you want to. Think about those people you might need to influence or those people you want to notice you.

Use the space overleaf to write a list of everyone you can think of who can help you with your career in some way.

The people who can help me are:

The following steps will help you to draw up a relationship map similar to the one illustrated on the next page.

Use the bubbles provided on page 202 to write in the names of the people you identified above. Write your name in the middle and place others either close or further away from you depending on how strong the relationship is currently.

Draw linking lines between the bubbles to show the relationships between each individual. Make any notes on the lines that show how they interact with you or each other.

Here's an example of what a relationship map might look like.

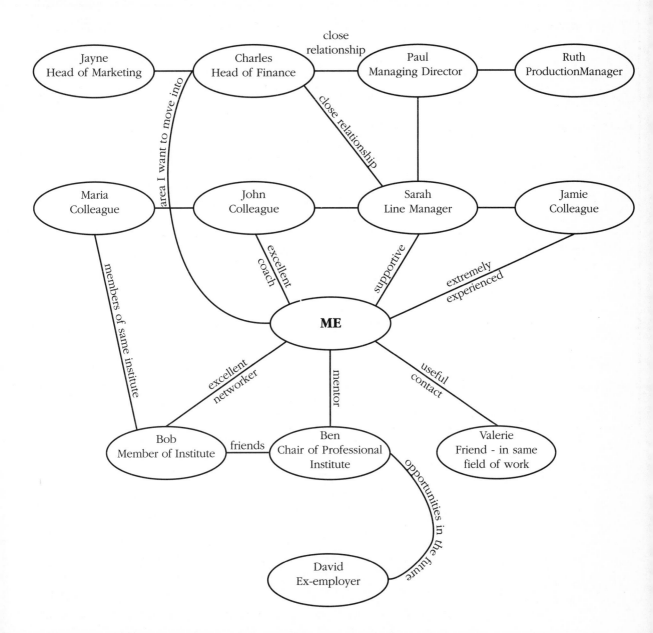

Use the empty bubbles to draw your relationship map.

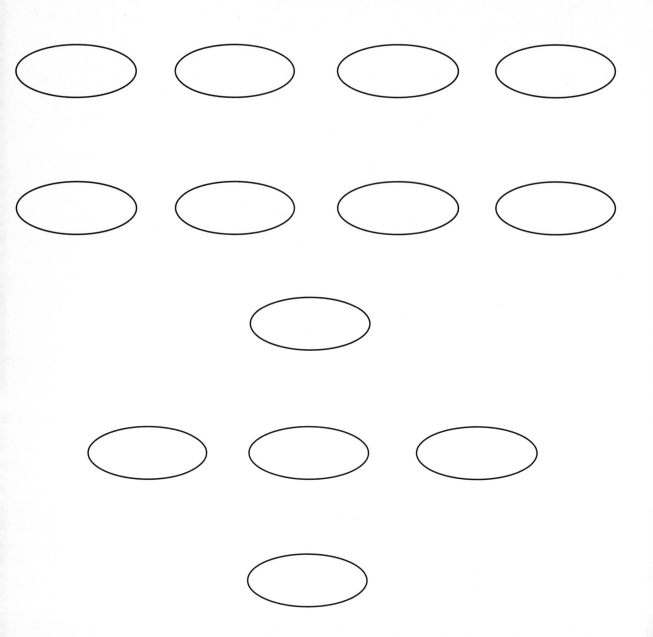

Look at your whole map.

> **ASK YOURSELF**

- Which relationships need strengthening?
- How can each person help me in going to work on my career?
- What do I give in return?

The last question, 'What do I give in return?' is a vital point to consider. In managing your career you are not working in isolation. You will need to give something back in return for what you want. In an employer/employee relationship this will be the work you do. When building individual relationships this may be slightly different and we will reflect on this later in this section when we look at networking.

111. Get noticed for the right reasons

Rebecca used a number of methods to get noticed which included:

- Canvassing companies.
- Volunteering to do tedious jobs.
- Raising her profile by instigating change.
- Getting involved in projects.
- Putting herself forward.

The important thing is to get noticed for a positive reason. It is also possible to get noticed for a negative reason. This might help someone remember you but not necessarily in a way you want them to. Getting noticed will mean that you will raise your profile within your company. Therefore, when an opportunity is on offer you will be remembered as the person right for that opportunity.

"Our aspirations are our possibilities."
Robert Browning

Let's consider other ways to get noticed for all the right reasons. Below, are some of the ways used by individuals we researched to get themselves noticed.

Getting noticed for the right reasons

- Coaching or training others.
- Presenting findings of research or reports.
- Contributing at meetings.
- Chairing meetings.
- Attending meetings not invited to, but at which they had a valuable contribution to make.
- Organising team or social events.
- Getting involved in charity work.
- Writing for the company newsletter.
- Asking to stand in for higher management at meetings.
- Personalising their workspace.
- Having positive quotes visible in workspace.
- Smiling at people.
- Approaching and talking to the right people.
- Putting forward ideas for improvements.
- Leading projects.
- Maintaining a high personal appearance.
- Introducing themselves to colleagues outside their immediate team.
- Being positive about change.

ASK YOURSELF

- What am I currently doing to get noticed?
- Are the right people noticing me?
- What else could I do to raise my profile?

112. Stray from the norm

In writing this book, Kathryn remembers a time when she took quite an unusual route to get herself noticed. She really wanted to present her ideas to the Managing Director regarding a new learning programme. However, it was impossible to get an appointment to see him as normally this direct route wouldn't have been the standard practice. She took to making sure he got to see her face on a regular basis so that he would recognise her. This involved being in corridors when he was walking by, in the car park and in the offices near his office. When she felt the time was right she caught him (actually coming back from the toilets) and struck up a conversation with him. This gave her the opportunity to outline her ideas and gain the next step forward, which was his agreement to meet to discuss it further.

**"Do what you can with what you have,
where you are."
Theodore Roosevelt**

No, we're not suggesting you loiter outside toilets! However, sometimes you might need to be a little creative and be prepared to do something slightly different to get noticed. It's back to the right person, right time - you might have to choose the right place!

113. Be a volunteer

If you want to raise your profile to help you along the road of your chosen career path, contemplate being a volunteer. You can volunteer to help others, get involved in projects, suggest ideas and do work that no one else wants to do. It's not about being a dogsbody. It's getting yourself recognised and adding value to the company you are working in.

**"You can get everything in life you want if you'll just
help enough other people get what they want."
Zig Ziglar**

You will have to find out what is happening in the organisation to know what to volunteer for. Rebecca talks about her 'radar', which she uses to detect opportunities. You can sharpen your radar by asking questions. Talk to people in other departments and find out what is happening. Make sure you read company literature, reports and newsletters. Never be scared to ask a question to discover what is happening – asking questions is another way of marketing yourself.

114. Add value

If you are volunteering to get involved you will need to know how you add value. What will the project, the meeting or others, gain from you being involved? You need to have a strong enough reason to take this action. Consider how you can help others to develop a strong enough reason to allow you to become involved.

**"You judge a person like you judge an apple tree,
by the fruit it produces."
Abraham Maslow**

PICK UP YOUR PEN

Look back to the section, **DEVELOP YOUR ABILITIES** (page 137 onwards) where you listed all your abilities. Consider how these abilities will help you add value to a range of situations and activities. Take this opportunity to write out a description of how you can add value.

I add value because:

Review your description:

- Ensure it is positively phrased (remember to build on your self-belief).
- Check it is an honest description.
- Ensure you have identified all the ways you can add value.

115.   Network, network and network

**"If you want to be prosperous for a year, grow grain.
If you want to be prosperous for ten years, grow trees.
If you want to be prosperous for a lifetime, grow people."
Proverb**

One of the most effective and successful ways to ensure you have contact with the right people and are remembered when opportunities emerge is to become an avid networker. This is different to the points raised in the earlier chapter, **BUILD A SUPPORT NETWORK** (page 163). Your support network consists of the people around you who constantly provide you with support on a personal level. We will be talking about networking in the context of expanding who you know and marketing yourself.

Some people are put off networking because they feel it means using others, feels forced and unnatural or means having to be aggressive to get yourself noticed. Networking is none of these things. Networking is getting to know people, through individuals or organisations you already know, for a specific purpose. It is also important to always be aware of what you offer in return. The successful networker always gives more than they get. What you give may be information, introductions, experience, practical help or advice.

"Getters don't get – givers get."
Eugene Benge

---

116. Identify opportunities for networking

Let's look at a few examples from the authors, of the different ways you can network. The focus is on how this can help you achieve success with your career.

Example one

Nicky had known her friend Joy for a number of years. Nicky was looking for a change of direction and a position which involved her expertise in psychology and research work, which she really loved. She had talked to a number of friends about her career aims, including Joy.

Joy worked for Go MAD Ltd. Andy, the Managing Director, happened to mention one day that he was looking to employ someone to do some research. Immediately Nicky sprang to Joy's mind. Nicky met with Andy, which resulted in Nicky being offered her ideal job. Along with Andy and Kathryn, she is now one of the authors of this book.

Nicky's example illustrates how friends are part of your network. Letting friends know what you want in your career can lead to opportunities.

ASK YOURSELF

- How clearly have I let my friends know my career aspirations?

Example two

Mike decided when attending an in-house career development programme in October that his current employer didn't offer him the career development opportunities he wanted so he set himself a goal:

'By January 31st, to receive an offer for a brilliant job, open it, smile and think 'Get In''.

Mike started applying for jobs and also contacted a previous manager, Brian, who he had really enjoyed working for, to see if there were any opportunities with his present company.

It got to 26th January and there was no job offer. He had visited Brian's company but then had a couple of meetings cancelled. He assumed there were no opportunities. Then out of the blue, Mike got a call from Brian offering him an exciting position. Guess what date the offer letter arrived – 31st January!

Keeping in touch with people, with whom you have worked in the past, is vital to successful networking. You may have moved on internally or externally, or they may have been the ones to make the move. This kind of networking will need to be more organised to maintain the relationship. It will mean that you will need to diarise in order to make regular contact with people you used to work with.

ASK YOURSELF

- Who have I worked with and how effectively have I kept in touch?
- Who do I want to keep in touch with?
- What could I do to ensure I keep in touch?

Example three

During a Go to Work on Your Career programme, Elise explained how she always went to her company's monthly communication forums. At these sessions she had the chance to talk to people she didn't usually see and find out what was happening in other parts of the business.

She happened to tell someone at one of these meetings about her wish to be able to move into a role where she could lead a team. A week later she got a call from a Head of Department offering her a secondment, to lead a team whilst the team leader was on maternity leave. The person she had spoken to at the meeting had passed on her name.

Meetings, forums, and professional institutes are all good places to network. They provide the opportunity to find out what is going on in your company or professional field. They are good places to meet people and to market yourself.

ASK YOURSELF

- What meetings, presentations or forums can I attend to extend my network?

"Knowledgeable people know facts. Successful and prosperous people know people."
John Demartini

---

117. Take eight steps to successful networking

The following eight steps, if followed, will guarantee the building and maintaining of an effective network.

Step one: Take every opportunity to develop contacts

Be aware of the people you meet on a day-to-day basis. How well are you building these relationships? How might they be able to help you? What can you offer them? How much do they know about your career aspirations?

Consider where you can go to widen your net. What meetings, forums or groups are available for you to attend? Find out who else goes to these meetings. What meetings or forums could you organise if there is currently nothing available?

Step two: Seek help

A great way of getting to know people is to ask for help. Most people love being asked for their advice or for information. Contrary to popular belief, most people like helping others when asked politely.

You can also ask for introductions to someone else. Everyone knows someone. Ensure you show and express appreciation for any help given.

Step three: Let people know the outcome of their help

Let the people know the outcome of the help they have given. A thank you note may be appropriate. They then know that you have taken some action as a result of their help.

Step four: Build the relationship beyond business

With some key contacts you may choose to put the relationship on more than a professional footing. It's okay to talk about topics which are not related to work in order to get to know people a bit better.

Steps five: Always give more than you get

Share information with others in your network. Let others know of opportunities that arise that may suit them. Give advice, help, information and introductions. Networking works both ways. Don't wait for someone else to help you; be the one to make the first step.

The people who have difficulty building a network are those that are in it solely for themselves. Bear in mind that whilst you may not be able to return help immediately, there will always be possibilities in the future.

Step six: Make contact with the right people

You can't network with everyone. However, the links in your network can make it a lot wider than it first seems. So don't try to get to know everyone. Make casual contact as the opportunities emerge. For more organised networking ensure you target people who can give you access to the information you need or access to others.

Step seven: Develop your networking skills

Practise introducing yourself to people. Practise what you will say. Identify topics you can introduce to the conversation. Think about the questions you can ask others to find out more about them. Taking an interest in others is the best way of taking pressure off you in networking situations. Identify what you feel comfortable, or uncomfortable, doing. What can you do to increase your level of comfort?

Having been introduced, remember to keep the relationship going with regular contact.

Step eight: Show you can be trusted

People in your network will trust you with information and relationships by introducing you to others. Always keep confidences and remember that your behaviour will reflect on the person who has made the introduction.

"A man learns in two ways, one by reading and the other by association with smarter people."
Will Rogers

---

118.   Expand your net

Stop to think about the number of people you know – 10, 20, 50, 100 plus? What do you think is the average number known to each individual? This includes family, friends, colleagues and work contacts. Even if you only know 20 people and those 20 know another 20 the total is already 420. What if of that 420, only 5% are useful contacts for your career? That could be at least 21 people to include in your network.

So, if you want to expand your network the simplest way is to talk to others about who they know, how well they know them and what they know about them. Sometimes the connections can be incredible. You may find out that one of your contacts knows the exact person you were wanting to meet. Expanding your network isn't necessarily about making it bigger; it's making sure it contains the right people. So, find out who knows who, and who you might want to get to know.

119.   Develop a script

Refer back to Rebecca's story at the beginning of the section. She spoke about developing 'a mental script of what she was going to say to people.' She was cold calling and she needed to have prepared what she was going to say, how she was going to introduce herself, and communicate her skills. Now, this can be the same with networking. What first impressions do you want to make by the way you introduce yourself? What are you going to say to get, and keep, the conversation going? We have found that it is the fear of what to say, that most puts people off networking.

"It is always a big person who walks up to you and offers his/her hand and says hello."
David J. Schwartz

One way of overcoming this fear is to do some preparation. Prepare how you will introduce yourself and identify questions you can ask to develop a conversation. If you are thinking this all sounds a bit false and over the top, compare it to going for a job interview. You would think through what you were going to say, how you were going to say it and the questions you wanted to ask. You never know, the person you are networking with might be a prospective employer or manager. So this could be the first step for a job interview – you can still be yourself and make the most of your personality.

120. Introduce yourself to create interest

Think about how you introduce yourself. What could you say to encourage the other person to want to talk to you? What first impression do you want to create? The key to introductions is to let people know who you are and what you do. It helps to include something that will help them to remember you. Compare these two introductions:

"Hello, I'm Nicky. I do research."

"Hello, I'm Nicky. I help others to increase their likelihood of making a difference by researching and sharing key success principles."

Now to you the second introduction might sound a bit unnatural. But not for Nicky – this is what she does. Let's face it. Someone is more likely to remember her from the second introduction as opposed to the first.

You need to find words that you are comfortable with and feel natural and easy to use, whilst at the same time creating a favourable impression.

> **"In walking just walk, in sitting just sit.**
> **Above all don't wobble."**
> **Yun-Men**

PICK UP YOUR PEN

It is now your chance to think about how you could be more creative in the way you introduce yourself. How can you ensure that when someone asks who you are, or what you do, your response has a positive lasting effect? Use the space below to write out several examples of self-introductions you feel comfortable with. We appreciate this might feel a bit awkward to do. But better to feel awkward in preparation, rather than in a real situation.

The ways I can introduce myself are:

Once you have written them, practise saying them out loud. How do they sound and feel? What are you most comfortable with? Make a decision about the self-introductions you will use.

> **"A simple interesting introduction is worth a thousand fancy words."**

To build on your introduction, think about the types of questions you can ask to maintain an interesting conversation. Ask people things they can talk about. For example, their work, their specific interests (in or out of work), their views on a specific work issue or how they obtained their current role. To increase your confidence, focus on asking questions and be interested (actually be interested as opposed to pretending to be interested). This will take the pressure off you and what you are going to say.

121. Present a positive image

You are marketing yourself in everything you say and do. An element of this will be your attitude to work and how that comes across to others. How often have you heard someone talking about another person and saying, *"They've got a real attitude problem."* It is important to recognise that our attitude or thoughts about situations, people and ourselves will affect what we say and do. So quite often when a person is talking about someone's attitude they are actually refering to the way they behave.

If an individual's attitude is that they are better than everyone else, then they will behave towards others in a condescending manner. Or, if an individual's attitude is that they just do enough to get by at work, they will not volunteer to help others and will earn little respect. Do you recognise either of these scenarios in your workplace?

> **"It ain't what you do, it's the way that you do it and that's what gets results"**
> **Fun Boy Three & Bananarama**

In relating this to career management we are coming at it from two angles. Firstly, how others interpret your attitude will impact on your image in the workplace and the effectiveness of your self-marketing. Secondly, your attitude to work will impact on how you go about managing your career.

Let's consider Rebecca's story and her attitude to work and her career. She goes after things; she is enthusiastic; she perseveres; she volunteers; and she is proactive. If this is her attitude, contemplate how this will show in her behaviour and how she comes across to others.

"Human beings can alter their lives by altering their attitudes of mind."
William James

Whether you like it or not, an element of managing your career will be how you come across to others. Think about these two scenarios:

John is unhappy with his work. He has been doing the same job for 10 years and is bored out of his brain. He doesn't want to change jobs as he earns good money and there is little progression apart from outside the company. He can do the job in his sleep and does just enough to get by. He can't be bothered with all this stuff about team working and team members being multi-skilled. John voices his disagreements loud and clear. Any changes that his manager introduces, he opposes and moans about to others.

Julia works on the same team. She has less experience than John but puts 100% effort into everything she does. She comes up with ideas for improved processes and procedures. She enjoys working in the team and has put together her own development plan to ensure she is developing in all the skill areas required of the team. She will challenge changes that are introduced in order to test their validity, but always gets involved in suggesting effective ways of implementation.

ASK YOURSELF

- Who would you rather work with?
- Who would you rather employ?
- Who would you consider involving if an opportunity arose?

We think we can guess your answers (all three questions answered Julia). This is just one example, however, it demonstrates how the impression we create through the attitude we display, can impact on success when going to work on your career.

PICK UP YOUR PEN

Take this opportunity to consider your own attitude to work. Imagine someone you have worked with or someone who knows you well is describing your attitude to work. What would they say? Use the box below to jot down your thoughts.

```
…………......................................attitude comes across as ……..
     (your name)




```

ASK YOURSELF

- How does my attitude to work help or hinder?
- How might it help or hinder in what I want to do with my career?
- What attitude and behaviours would I like to develop?
- Who controls my attitude and how I behave?

The key question above is, 'Who controls my attitude and how I behave?' Hopefully, you will recognise that your attitude and behaviour is fully within your control. Hence, you can choose what image you want to present. If you feel that at times this is difficult look back to the section **BELIEVE IN YOURSELF** (page 105). There you will find some hints and tips on how to develop different attitudes by focusing on your beliefs.

If you don't like your work you have two options:
    1. **Change your job**
    2. **Change your attitude**

CAPTURE YOUR THOUGHTS

Having reached the end of this section take some time to relate your situation to the points that have emerged from Rebecca's story. Make a note of any points you want to remember and summarise any action you want to take. Consider:

- How effectively have I been marketing myself?
- What more could I do?
- What is the current state of my network?
- How much do I stand out from the crowd?

PERSONAL THOUGHTS AND REFLECTIONS

THREE ACTIONS FOR YOU TO CONSIDER

Here are three suggested actions to help you market yourself effectively.

1. Plan to get in touch with all your network contacts over the next two months.

2. Make two new contacts (who will be helpful in going to work on your career) in the next three months. Make one in the next week. Use your newly developed self-introduction script.

3. Observe the attitude of others to their work and career. What impression does it present? Compare this with the impression you want to give.

TELL YOUR STORY

The story of Brigideen McGuire

Brigideen started her working life, aged thirteen, as a Saturday girl in a bookshop in her local town of Corby. She left full time education at fifteen with no clear career aspirations. Over the next four years Brigideen experienced many different roles. Twelve months of this period were spent in Jersey where she was employed, amongst other things, as a waitress and potato picker!

After returning from Jersey, Brigideen moved to London where she registered with an employment agency. A variety of clerical roles followed. At the age of nineteen, she began full time employment at a garage. Initially Brigideen was employed as an administrative assistant, however, she quickly progressed to the role of office manager.

Brigideen found this role both stimulating and interesting, she gained broad experience in all aspects of management. She describes the owner of the garage as an excellent role model, and a great businessman. Brigideen honed her communication and negotiation skills over a short period of time. She earned her bosses respect and trust, and was involved in many different aspects of business. At the suggestion of the garage proprietor, Brigideen decided to go back to college to re-sit her maths 'O' Level and complete an 'O' Level in Accounts. However, she was still unsure of what she wanted to do. When the owner of the car dealership retired, Brigideen was prompted into reassessing her needs and aspirations.

Brigideen made the move back to her hometown of Corby. Feeling ready for a change, she knew she didn't want an office management role. However, she found it difficult to get prospective employers to take a leap of faith and trust that she was capable of doing other roles. As a consequence, Brigideen ended up becoming a Customer Services Manager for a Dutch company. They needed somebody to run the office. Her role turned out to be more like that of a 'Girl Friday', with only a little people management involved. This role came to an end when the company decided to relocate. Brigideen, pregnant with her second child, made the decision to stay in Corby and look for a different role.

Brigideen took a break from her career to concentrate on her growing family. However, after a period of twelve months she became restless and anxious to get back to work. She missed the company and stimulation of working life.

As Brigideen's husband worked shifts, she had to consider what kind of employment would fit in with her family life. A job arose as a charge hand supervisor on a production line. This fitted in with Brigideen's criteria for work. The job's hours suited her and the wage was good.

However, she felt little satisfaction in her work. Nevertheless, Brigideen looked for opportunities which would enable her to progress up the supervisory hierarchy and earn more money. She observed her immediate supervisors, told herself she could do the same job better, and approached her manager asking for a promotion. This occurred several times, with Brigideen progressing through the ranks until she was offered the assistant production manager's job. However, she declined the position, as it was full time shift work and she was aware that this type of supervision wasn't what she wanted to do for the rest of her working life.

The acknowledgement that she didn't enjoy factory supervision prompted Brigideen to seek employment in an office environment. This, however, was easier said than done. Despite her substantial experience, as the mother of two children, with few academic qualifications to speak of, she experienced difficulties in finding appropriate work. She decided to apply for a job in the same company for whom she had worked when she was sixteen. Much to Brigideen's surprise they offered her a job in customer services. To begin with, a majority of Brigideen's work consisted of telephone enquires. However, she quickly began to observe her immediate supervisors and looked for ways to progress.

After speaking to her brother who worked in RS Components, Brigideen decided that she wanted to work there too. Brigideen felt that RS Components were a company that would offer her the opportunity to experience different roles and support her personal development. Gaining access to such a prestigious company was to prove challenging. However, she knew that if she could get her foot in the door she could impress.

She carried out a little research and found out that the company occasionally used temping agencies for their office staff. So she registered with the appropriate agency. After a short time they offered her a temporary purchasing position at RS Components. She temped at the company for a couple of weeks and remained confident that she could make a difference to the department. At the end of the three week temporary contract Brigideen was offered a permanent contract of twelve months.

Almost as soon as she began her permanent contract, Brigideen began looking around at her immediate supervisors, observing and assessing what they did. She consistently sought jobs with more responsibility, either applying for them as they arose or by approaching her manager and asking for a change of role. *"If you believe that you can do something, then do it. When I know and believe I can do something, then I can be very 'pushy' and I will actively seek a role."*

Academically Brigideen started with nothing. However, the lack of qualifications made her all the more determined to impress. Eighteen months ago Brigideen decided to enroll at college on a DMS (Diploma in Management Studies). With the help and support of her manager, Brigideen sought, and won, financial support from RS Components.

Her lack of qualifications meant that Brigideen also had to fight to gain a place on the DMS. She had to have an interview, followed by an entrance test which she found very tough. Despite her questionable test results, her enthusiasm shone through and she was offered a place on the course. Brigideen acknowledges that she began the DMS, not to ensure promotion – she felt that sheer effort would ensure she was promoted – but rather to increase her self-confidence and belief. It has also taught her other skills and disciplines including report writing, structure, self-discipline, and how to communicate and articulate her ideas.

At the same time, Brigideen also sought a new challenge within RS Components. She decided that she wanted to experience a sales role. She made an appointment with the Sales Director and enquired to see what roles would be available to her. After a stimulating conversation, where Brigideen made it clear that whatever she lacked in experience she more than made up for in enthusiasm, she was offered an interview for a Corporate Account Manager's job. As a testament to her personal persuasiveness, Brigideen was the only person outside of the sales department who was offered an interview for the position.

Unfortunately, she was unsuccessful in her application. Nevertheless Brigideen felt that she had impressed the Sales Director. She was told that when a vacancy arose for a Key Account Manager she would be invited for an interview. However, yet another obstacle arose for her when the Sales Director, with whom she had spent so much time discussing her career needs, left the company. She was very concerned that his replacement would not share the same views and wouldn't consider someone outside of the sales department for interview.

A short while later, Brigideen found out that the original job she'd applied for remained vacant. She did further homework and decided it was time to speak to the new Sales Director. Without making an appointment (Brigideen felt that she had waited long enough), she knocked on the Director's door early one morning with a proposal for him. She asked him to give her a trial period as a Corporate Account Manager, with no salary or grade increase. She insisted that she could do the job very well and deserved this chance.

After some deliberation, Brigideen received a phone call – her wish had come true! At the time of this interview, Brigideen was successfully managing a large corporate account. She describes success as, *"Happiness in what you do,"* Brigideen argues that what you need is enthusiasm, motivation, determination to succeed and the ability to be industrious.

"It takes a thousand voices to tell a single story."
Native American Saying

---

122. Reflect on the past

You have just read Brigideen's story. The story of her career, from starting work to present day. The purpose of this section is for you to think about the story of your career. This will help focus on what you have learnt and how you want to move forward.

PICK UP YOUR PEN

The rest of this page and the next page have been left blank for you to write the story of your career. Start at whatever point you consider your career began. This is just for you, so there are no prizes for the best grammar and spelling!

The story of ....
           (insert your name)

**"The most important time of one's life is now –
right now."
Tony Curtis**

ASK YOURSELF

From my story:

- What have been my key experiences in managing my career?
- What have I learnt about managing my career from my experiences?
- What have been the best bits?
- Why were these the best bits?

If you don't learn from the past you will repeat it.

123. Look to the future

Having reflected on the past take some time to look to the future. The rest of this page and the next page have been left blank for you to write the story of your future career. You can decide how far forward you describe. You have two options. You can write from the present and describe your future, or you can imagine yourself in the future looking back and describing your past career. The choice is yours.

The future of ....
        (insert your name)

"The best thing about the future is that it comes only one day at a time."
Abraham Lincoln

ASK YOURSELF

- What are the reasons I want my future to be like this?
- How strong are these reasons?
- What am I doing to create the future?
- What do I believe about the achievability of the future I described?

"Life is not a problem to be solved but a gift to be enjoyed."
Source Unknown

PLAN YOUR WAY FORWARD

The story of Mike Waterfield

We met Mike when he attended one of our Go to Work on Your Career programmes about three years ago. He was then a senior player in a firm of accountants. He had been with the company from its inception – 14 years in total.

Mike had built up a good client base and had formed strong relationships with all of his customers. He saw his position within the organisation as very strong. However, unbeknown to Mike, changes were afoot. Quite unexpectedly, Mike and his colleagues were informed that the business was being sold!

The new proprietor of the business was fairly relaxed in his attitudes and demands. However, Mike found himself with additional responsibilities. He was expected to increase both his workload and his people management roles.

After managing this change for a short time, the realisation that he was employed in the same position, with many additional responsibilities, prompted Mike to consider his career options.

As Mike saw it, he had three fundamental options available to him; he could approach his new boss and discuss a possible partnership; he could look for employment in another firm; or he could fulfil a lifetime ambition and set up his own business.

Initially Mike put option one into place and approached his boss. Discussions led to the fact that there wasn't a partnership available at this time. Following this somewhat disappointing response, and after careful consideration, Mike made the decision to follow his ambition and set up in business for himself.

Having decided on his goal, Mike began to put plans into place. His first move was to invite a colleague to partner him in his new business venture. In the initial stages of setting up his business, Mike identified all the possible obstacles he might face including the financial implications of being self-employed and the practicalities of establishing a strong client base. He put plans into place to overcome these obstacles. Fortunately Mike's previous dedication to customer satisfaction paid off and a vast majority of his client base transferred their alliance to his new business!

Mike set himself a number of subgoals under the framework of his primary goal to own a thriving accountancy business. Mike knew he and his business partner had the abilities and the drive to get this business venture off the ground. They believed that their goal was achievable. After identifying and prioritising possible actions, Mike and his partner put together an action plan. Then the most important thing – they started to implement their action plan.

The business grew beyond Mike's wildest expectations! Mike and his partner have consistently reviewed their goals: reassessing their position; putting into action plans to employ the right people in the business; and establishing a robust infrastructure. At this present time Mike chooses to place considerable amounts of time and effort into creating a strong and secure client base. However, despite the huge support he receives from his wife, he feels that his life balance is currently out of shape. He all too frequently finds himself working evenings and weekends in order to keep on top of his workload. Mike has committed to review this at the end of the year, he then plans to readdress the balance.

His commitment to prioritising, planning and taking action is reflected in Mike's resounding success.

"Some succeed because they are destined to, but most succeed because they are determined to."
Source Unknown

---

124. Pull it all together

Here we are nearly at the end of the book. This is the session where it gets serious – where you can decide to take your career seriously (if you haven't already). We hope that by the end of this section you have committed to paper some actions you will take to Go to Work on Your Career. We will pull out points from Mike's story to help you with action planning. We encourage you to review the previous sections of the book. So it's decision time. Do you want to plan to:

- Ensure you take responsibility for your career?
- Ensure your career is what you want it to be?
- Remain employable in a changing world?
- Maintain and develop transferable skills?
- Increase your value in the workplace?

- Focus on what is really important to you?
- Achieve your balance of life?
- Increase your job satisfaction?
- Get the most out of your time at work?

If not – that's your choice. If yes let's get on with it!

"Having a dream isn't stupid, Norm.
It's not having a dream that's stupid."
Cliff Clavin (TV show – Cheers)

---

125.   Continue to learn from others

Let's take a few moments to pick up on the key points from Mike's story about the actions he took to draw together his Go to Work on Your Career Action Plan. Mike took the following steps in putting his plan in place:

- He set himself some goals, some of which were broken down into subgoals.
- He was sure of his reasons for wanting to achieve these goals.
- He believed that it was possible for him to achieve these goals.
- He believed he was capable of achieving his goals (in fact he has exceeded them).
- He identified all the possibilities before taking action.
- When he had decided on his course of action he prioritised the possible steps he could take.
- He involved others in identifying possibilities and helping him to achieve his goals.
- He formulated his ideas into a plan.
- He identified potential obstacles and planned to overcome them.
- He was willing to be accountable for the success or failure of his plans.
- He set himself further goals once initial goals were achieved.

- He has planned time to review his goals and plans – specifically how they affect his life balance.

By taking these steps Mike was setting himself up to succeed. Not suprisingly, he did succeed. He followed through on his plan and took action.

"The quality of life is determined by it's activities."
Aristotle

---

126. Review before planning

We suggest that you undertake a review before jumping straight into putting together an action plan. Allow yourself the opportunity to capture all the thoughts and ideas raised when reading the book.

In chapter 134 (page 240) we have put together a framework for an action plan. This will be your personal Go to Work on Your Career Action Plan. This is only a suggestion. If you prefer a different structure to your action plan, feel free to adapt it.

The next seven chapters (pages 233 to 240) will help you to identify information for your action plan. You might feel that this is a lot of time and effort to put together an action plan. Well, we think you're worth it. You are planning an important area of your life. It needs thought, time and effort because – you are important!

"There are three things extremely hard.
Steel, a diamond, and to know one's self."
Benjamin Franklin

---

127. Review your reason why

Review the book section, **FIND YOUR REASON WHY** (page 33). Look back and remind yourself of your reasons for managing your career.

ASK YOURSELF

- What can I build into my action plan to ensure that I keep reminding myself of my reason for going to work on my career?

Use this space to make any notes:

128. Reflect on what is important to you

Turn back to the book section **DECIDE WHAT IS IMPORTANT TO YOU** (page 47). Consider the elements you decided were important to you.

ASK YOURSELF

- How will my action plan reflect my personal values?
- What do I need to build into my action plan to ensure job satisfaction?
- What do I need to build into my action plan to meet my personal definition of success?

Use this space to make any notes:

129. Go for a balanced life

You will understand the pattern of this section now – go back to the **ACHIEVE A BALANCE** (page 65) section of the book. Focus on what a balanced life means for you.

ASK YOURSELF

- How can I make sure I achieve the balance I want in my life?
- How can this be reflected in my action plan?

Use this space to make any notes:

130. Identify your key goal areas

Now take some time to review the following sections of the book:

- **DEFINE YOUR GOALS**   – page 81
- **BELIEVE IN YOURSELF**   – page 105
- **DEVELOP YOUR ABILITIES**   – page 133
- **CREATE OPPORTUNITIES**   – page 175
- **MARKET YOURSELF**   – page 195
- **TELL YOUR STORY**   – page 221

Look back through the activities undertaken and consider the thoughts and ideas raised. As you go through the sections, make a note of the areas of your work or life in which you want to make a difference. You may well have already identified some of these in the section **DEFINE YOUR GOALS** (page 81).

Examples of the key areas to consider are:
- Work roles
- Work experience
- Personal development
- Financial
- Family
- Building relationships
- Well-being (health and fitness)
- Contribution (how you help others)
- Travel
- Job satisfaction
- Life roles – Manager, Mother, Father, Spouse, Friend, Colleague

PICK UP YOUR PEN

Make a note of likely areas of your career and life around which you want to define some goals. Decide what you will call these areas – give them a title.

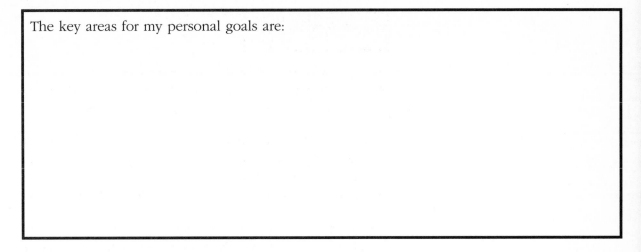

The key areas for my personal goals are:

Now, turn to chapter 133 (page 240) and note these key areas on your Go to Work on Your Career Action Plan.

131. Write down your goals

Having identified the areas for your personal goals, let's get some goals written down. Before doing this, look back to the section **DEFINE YOUR GOALS** (page 101) where you were given the opportunity to write some personal goals. Use that section to remind yourself of the key points in effective goal setting.

PICK UP YOUR PEN

Turn to your Go to Work on Your Career Action Plan (page 241). Use the space provided to write down your personal goals. Categorise them under the appropriate key headings. Remember:

● To make them SMART.
● To break any bigger goals into subgoals. Write your subgoals in the space provided.
● To include time scales.
● To describe specifically what it is you want to achieve.

Once you have written them look at each goal and:

ASK YOURSELF

- Do I believe these goals are achievable?
- Do I believe I have the abilities, or can develop the abilities, to achieve these goals?

If either of your answers to these questions is no, reassess your goals. You have two choices. Either change your goals to something you believe is achievable or plan to increase your self-belief, which can become a goal in itself.

"Real generosity towards the future consists in giving all to what is present."
Albert Camus

132. Identify possibilities

Time to really start planning. Begin with identifying all the possible actions to take to achieve your goals or sub goals. Notice we say **possible**. At this stage just think about **all** the things you **could** do. You can determine definite actions later.

PICK UP YOUR PEN

For each goal or subgoal list the possible actions you could take.

Bear in mind the following pointers when identifying possibilities.

- Go for many possibilities – this will give you plenty of choice.
- Include all ideas – even if they seem a bit wacky.
- Break any bigger actions into smaller actions.
- Identify likely obstacles. Identify actions to overcome these obstacles and add these to your possibilities.

- Include actions that will support the balance you want to achieve in your life.
- Remember to include possible actions about maintaining momentum. For example, how to remind yourself of your reasons why and take time to review your plans.
- Identify who could help and how. What action will you take to involve them? It might help if you review the book sections **BUILD A SUPPORT NETWORK** (page 163) and **MARKET YOURSELF** (page 195). This will help you identify who will be there to support you and who you want to include in your career network.
- Identify the possible resources needed to take these actions. List the actions needed to get hold of these resources. (These are all possible actions.)
- Keep going until you have exhausted all possibilities.

Goals List your goals and subgoals	Actions List all possible actions to achieve each goal

133. Prioritise and plan

The next stage is to prioritise the actions to be taken. Actions are usually prioritised on the basis of urgent and important. Urgent being those actions that need doing immediately; important being those actions that are critical to your goals being achieved.

PICK UP YOUR PEN

Go back to your list of possibilities. Look at each one and decide whether it is:

- urgent and important
- important but not urgent
- not important or urgent

Make a note at the side of each action.

This should now give you the priority of your actions:

- The actions identified as neither urgent nor important will not need including in your action plan.
- Those that are urgent and important will need doing first. Put them at the top of the list.
- Those that are important but not urgent will follow.

Now, go to your Go to Work on Your Career Action Plan and write in your actions in priority order. Write the date the action is to be taken for each point.

134. Go to Work on Your Career Action Plan

Your action plan is spread over several pages to allow you to include all the key areas that make up your career. As we said earlier, you do not have to use this plan. Action plans are personal things so feel free to develop your own format.

KEY AREA:	KEY AREA:
GOALS	**GOALS**
SUBGOALS	**SUBGOALS**
ACTIONS	**ACTIONS**

KEY AREA:	KEY AREA:
GOALS	**GOALS**
SUBGOALS	**SUBGOALS**
ACTIONS	**ACTIONS**

KEY AREA:	KEY AREA:
GOALS	**GOALS**
SUBGOALS	**SUBGOALS**
ACTIONS	**ACTIONS**

135. Ensure it happens

It's all well and good having a fantastic, well-written plan. For the plan to be effective you will need to take action. Our research uncovered the following tips to help in ensuring action is taken:

- Share your plan with someone. Actually say them out loud. They become more real.
- Keep it visible. Keep your plan somewhere you can see it on a daily basis.
- Remember it is not set in concrete. Be flexible. Be willing to change timescales and take different actions as opportunities emerge.
- Put timescales on the actions. Diarise the actions to be taken.
- Set a date to review your plan.
- Ensure your self-talk supports you taking action. Talk to yourself about what you are going to do.
- Enjoy following the plan. Don't be a slave to it. Remind yourself of your reasons why on a regular basis.
- Recognise achievements. Reward yourself when you have taken an action or achieved a goal. Give yourself a treat.
- Remember this isn't extra work. You would be at work anyway – so why not be working towards what it is you want?

"If you must begin then go all the way, because if you begin and quit, the unfinished business you have left behind begins to haunt you all the time."
Chögyam Trungpa

---

136. Time to say goodbye

We have nearly reached the end of this book. We hope that you have gained what you wanted when you picked it up. We hope it has encouraged you to give some time to yourself and your career. Remember this doesn't have to be a one-off activity. Plan to do this on a regular basis.

At the beginning of the book we said that on average people spend more time planning their holidays than they do planning their careers. If you have read the book, done some of the activities and formulated your Go to Work on Your Career Action Plan you will have put yourself into a small percentage of the population. The small percentage that thinks about and plans their working life. So, have fun, enjoy what work gives you and above all continue to Go to Work on Your Career.

"Enjoy yourself. These are the good old days that you might miss in the years ahead."

---

137.   Find the actions that relate to you

Each section of the book ends with three suggested actions that will help you to implement the learning from that section.

These actions are listed below under section headings for easy reference.

DEFINE YOUR CAREER

1. Talk to others (friends, family, colleagues, or anyone who will talk to you) about their careers. Focus on how they define their career. Compare this with how you define your career.
2. Put a date in your diary to review the activities in this chapter once you have read the whole of the book. The date you give yourself will depend on how quickly you read.
3. Carry on reading the book, considering the questions put to you, and doing the activities.

FIND YOUR REASON WHY

1. Write down your reasons for managing your career and put them somewhere you can see them every day.
2. Look back over your career and identify if there is a pattern of you either being motivated towards a goal, or away from a problem. If the motive for action has usually been away from, start to think about what you might be motivated towards.
3. Decide if your reason for managing your career is strong enough. If not, think of ways you can make it stronger.

DECIDE WHAT IS IMPORTANT TO YOU

1. Write a description of the job that would encompass all the factors you have identified as being important to you. How does this compare with your current job?
2. If you are in a long-term relationship, ask your partner

to complete the life priorities activity. Take some time to discuss what is important to both of you and how your personal priorities impact on each other.

3. Consider how your personal values have been formed. What and who has influenced you? What is likely to influence you in the future? How will this impact on your career?

ACHIEVE A BALANCE

1. Talk to people close to you about the balance they want in their life. How does this fit with what you want? Discuss how their needs impact on the life balance you want.

2. Pick three actions from the managing pressure ideas list (pages 74-75). Take these actions at least once over the next week. Reinforce these actions as a habit, by doing them over and over again.

3. Put a date in your diary for the next time you will review your life balance.

DEFINE YOUR GOALS

1. Write your goals out again. Put them somewhere you can see them on a regular basis.

2. Imagine what your life would be like when you have achieved your goals. Have a good daydream – picture it in detail.

3. Decided on the positive messages you can say internally to keep you focused on your goals. Write them down and regularly say them to yourself.

BELIEVE IN YOURSELF

1. Write a list of things you like about yourself. Plan to do this at least every three months.

2. Pick a situation where you would like to be more confident. Use the information in this section to be well prepared. Go for it!

3. Talk to yourself nicely every day.

DEVELOP YOUR ABILITIES

1. Update, or produce, your C.V. to include all your recent achievements and newly developed abilities.
2. Each week review what you have learnt (however insignificant). Consciously identify and record your learning experiences.
3. Research the changes likely to impact on your organisation and your career. Read relevant information, keep abreast of the job market and talk to others.

BUILD A SUPPORT NETWORK

1. Discuss your career aspirations with your manager. Discuss ways he or she can support you in going to work on your career.
2. Thank those people who have supported, or still support, you. A bit of appreciation goes a long way.
3. Act on the areas in which you lack support. Approach others and ask for help.

CREATE OPPORTUNITIES

1. Research areas for improvement within your organisation. Identify options to be researched in more depth.
2. Review the opportunities that have come your way over the last two years. Identify the action you took to make the most of these opportunities. Identify what more you could have done to make the most of these opportunities.
3. If you ever hear yourself complaining about work, recognise the choices you are making. If you don't like what is happening, identify what choices you have. Choose whether or not you want to act on these choices.

MARKET YOURSELF

1. Plan to get in touch with all your network contacts over the next two months.
2. Make two new contacts (who will be helpful on going to work on your career) in the next three months. Make one in the next week. Use your newly developed self-introduction script.
3. Observe the attitude of others to their work and career. What impression does it present? Compare this with the impression you want to give.

"The best prize life offers is the chance to work hard at work worth doing."
Theodore Roosevelt

---

138. Index of stories

The case-studies we have used in the book are indexed below. Feel free to browse the list and go straight to those that interest you. Read and enjoy the inspirational message they tell.

Margaret Burke
One2One
FIND YOUR REASON WHY   33

Sarah Armitage
Acordis Acetates
DECIDE WHAT IS IMPORTANT TO YOU   47

Carl Robley
One2One
ACHIEVE A BALANCE   65

Helen Bunbury
Royal and SunAlliance
DEFINE YOUR GOALS   81

Darren Brooker
One2One
BELIEVE IN YOURSELF   105

Nigel Beard
Acordis Acetates
DEVELOP YOUR ABILITIES   133

Ken Bew
RS Components
BUILD A SUPPORT NETWORK   163

Mark Christer
Royal and SunAlliance
CREATE OPPORTUNITIES   175

Rebecca Denning-Southern
Royal and SunAlliance
MARKET YOURSELF   195

Brigideen McGuire
RS Components
TELL YOUR STORY   221

Mike Waterfield
Torr Waterfield
PLAN YOUR WAY FORWARD   229

139. Go MAD® information

If you would like to receive more information about other books in the Go MAD® range or details of other Go MAD® personal and business development products.

OR

If you are looking for new, inspiring, practical ways to develop yourself or your organisation, we offer a range of innovative Go MAD® training solutions, conference speakers, personal coaches and consultancy options.

Contact the Go MAD® team:

Go MAD Ltd
Pocket Gate Farm
Off Breakback Road
Woodhouse Eaves
Leicestershire
LE12 8RS

01509 891313

www.gomadonline.com

info@gomadonline.com

Other Go MAD® books include:

Go MAD – The Art of Making A Difference
(by Andy Gilbert)
The best selling Go MAD® personal development book that explains the 7 Go MAD® key principles indepth. It contains plenty of exercises and inspirational quotations to help you focus on making a difference and increasing your success.

Go MAD About Coaching
(by Andy Gilbert & Ian Chakravorty)
This pragmatic book demonstrates step by step how the Go MAD® process can easily be used as a framework to successfully coach yourself and others. It contains over 200 powerful coaching questions, 120 tips, tools and techniques and templates of how to structure a coaching session. It also includes a free audio C.D. containing 60 minutes of coaching examples and exercises.

Yes! I Can Make A Difference
(by Andy Gilbert)
A book with a difference - it hasn't been fully written yet! It contains 234 inspirational quotes and high quality questions – and lots of space for you to write in. An ideal notebook, personal diary or success journal – you choose.

Go MAD® About Meetings – 87 Ways to Make A Difference
(by Andy Gilbert & Alison Lawrence)
A handy tips booklet that provides practical ideas about applying the Go MAD® process to preparing and running meetings. Guaranteed to save time and provide focus.

Contagious Customer Care
(by Nicky Frisby, Ian Chakravorty & Alison Lawrence)
A book of practical ways to make a difference when providing customer service. It contains case-studies and inspirational stories, together with hints and tips that combine to help you consider how to Go MAD® about customer care in your organisation or team.

59 Minutes to a Calmer Life
(by Paul McGee)
Practical strategies for reducing stress in your personal and professional life. This easy to read book is packed full of common sense, good humour, helpful advice and useful insights to help you make a difference in your life.

Go MAD® Audio products include:

The Complete Guide to Making A Difference
(by Andy Gilbert)
A six tape box set which covers everything you need to know about Go MAD® and its uses as a development process, a diagnostic tool and an analytical framework. Understand and increase your ability to apply the 7 Go MAD® key principles to develop yourself, others and your organisation. Features extracts from the original research interviews.

Go MAD® about Coaching
(by Andy Gilbert)
A six tape box set which demonstrates the powerful Go MAD® Coaching process and will increase your ability to successfully coach others. Understand the Go MAD® Framework in greater depth and how to structure a coaching session using high quality questions. Plenty of examples, tips and techniques are demonstrated and explained.

The Go MAD® Monthly Audio Magazine
A monthly source of inspiration and practical ideas to help you Go MAD®. Features the latest Go MAD® research interviews with successful people from a variety of backgrounds; development exercises; and insights from Andy Gilbert about how to apply the Go MAD® process to your life and work. This provides ideal support and further development following Go MAD® Training.

Go MAD® Corporate Development Programmes include:

Go MAD® Accredited Programmes
A series of six consecutive training programmes each of which builds upon previous Go MAD® knowledge and experience to develop a high level of conscious competence in applying the Go MAD® process.

Part 1 – Yes! I Can Make A Difference   (2 days)
Part 2 – Go MAD® about Coaching   (2 days)
Part 3 – Go MAD® about Meetings and Projects (1 day)

(Parts 1, 2 and 3 are often combined to form a bespoke 4 day Accredited Coach Programme.)

Part 4 – Go MAD® Leadership Programme   (4 days over
                                                                          6 months)
Part 5 – Go MAD® Mindset Programme   (2^1/2 days)
Part 6 – Go MAD® Master Coach/Trainer   (5 days)
          Programme

Go MAD® Trainer Training for in-house licensed programmes

Parts 1,2 and 3 of the Accredited Programmes can be run internally with a license to reproduce copyright materials and use Go MAD® training videos featuring key learning points by Andy Gilbert.

Bespoke workshops and courses

These are designed to apply the Go MAD®process to specific issues that teams or organisations want to make a difference about. Recent examples include: culture change; customer care; sales; stress; career management; leadership.

Go MAD® Intranet Learning

Over 18 hours of interactive online learning about Go MAD. The ultimate support tool with the functionality to electronically network and involve others within your organisation in the differences people want to make. It contains an artificial intelligence coaching programme to coach individuals using Go MAD® process, together with a management information system to measure the success of your training e-development activities.

Go MAD® ongoing research and development includes:
- Success profiling and a range of Go MAD® assessment tools
- Digital interactive television and e-learning
- Masterclass tele-conferencing

For current information or to be kept up to date on any of the above mentioned Go MAD® products, services or development areas please contact us and we will endeavour to help you make a difference.

If you would like to involve others in making a difference, visit the website:

www.principlefive.com

On this site you will be able to network with other people interested in making a difference. Register free to obtain a weekly Go MAD® inspirational quotation.